PRAISE FO

"What a wonderful and timely book! In all my years of working with financial professionals, the brilliant Abe Abich has been among a handful of special advisors who truly understand how getting "down the mountain" of retirement planning requires a different approach and mindset than the journey up. An absolute must-read for retirees, those about to retire, and anyone who wants to see Americans retire safely and securely".

> Joel Tabin, CLU, ChFC, AEP
> Regional Sales Director
> Midland National Life

"Abe deconstructs the complex and intimidating financial maze into an easy-to-follow guide to navigating your dream retirement. If you're someone whose eyes glaze over at the discussion of investments or are so fearful of making the wrong financial decision that you freeze over, this book can help you gain the quiet confidence to conquer your fears. This is a must-read if you want to learn from one of the best in the business!"

> Evan Ward
> Founder
> Atlas Retirement

"If you're looking for a clear, actionable guide to secure a fulfilling and financially stable retirement, *The Retirement Mountain: The 7 Steps to a Long Lasting Retirement* is the book for you. With practical steps and thoughtful insights, this book makes the path to a successful retirement both achievable and inspiring. A must-read for anyone serious about their financial future and long-term happiness!"

>Thomas Zebley
>President
>Impact Partnership

"In a world full of uncertainty, this book can help you to make your retirement plan more certain. If you are nearing or in retirement, this is a must-read! It's one thing to grow your money, and it's another to have it last a lifetime and to protect it from all of the uncertainties in the world."

>Chris Hoffman
>Founder and President
>Hoffman Financial Group

"Abe's book on retirement offers a fresh and insightful perspective on planning for the next chapter of life. Packed with practical advice and thought-provoking strategies, it's a must-read for anyone looking to transition into retirement with confidence and purpose."

>Stephen Odom
>Chief Executive Officer
>Impact Partnership

"When you combine an intelligent man of integrity with focus and a love of helping people conquer the mountain of retirement, you get Abe Abich. In all my dealings with Abe he has been honest, thoughtful, caring, and willing to go the second mile. He's also creative and when it comes to money management - that's a rare plus!"

    Pam Pryor
    Strength Finders Coach

"*The Retirement Mountain* offers a straight forward, empowering roadmap for anyone seeking lasting financial security. I believe this book helps to serve as the compass to help individuals navigate this every so important journey called retirement".

    Brad Jenkins
    CEO & Founder of Market Guard

"You can find retirement advice anywhere you look, but let's face it, you rarely see a clear and concise approach to retirement planning. In *The Retirement Mountain*, Abe breaks down the fundamentals of retirement into an easy-to-follow format that empowers you to better understand your retirement options. To say this should be added to the must-read list for retirees is an understatement! It's a definite read for anyone retired or nearing retirement!"

    Jim Fox
    President and Founder
    Wadadli Financial Group

"There are many risks in retirement facing baby boomers today. Running out of money, excessive market swings, increasing taxes, legislative changes, increasing health and LTC costs. Abe's passion for planning, managing risk and love for his clients' financial well being is unmatched in the financial services industry. His dedication to his clients is matched by his dedication to his family, faith and endurance hiking pursuits. It is impressive watching him empty his tank hiking on the mountain to complete his goals. This same drive is shown in his daily commitment to his clients' financial wellbeing. This book is a must read for anyone concerned about retirement risks and how to protect against them".

>Adam Wolf CPA, CFP®
>Wolf Retirement Navigation

"*The Retirement Mountain* does a masterful job of explaining how retirement planning SHOULD be done. Abe provides practical strategies for financial security while emphasizing that retirement planning is about more than numbers-its about protecting the people you love."

>Joshua E. Hummer, Esq.
>Relational Estate & Elder Law

"What an incredible book sharing an incredible journey. Keeping with the climbing a mountain analogy, it is so easy to get caught up in all the noise—either the wind blowing on the top of a mountain or the financial noise you find on tv, the internet, and social media. The beauty of taking that first step with Abe and his team, is they teach you to stop and listen to the quietness. Abe aptly points out that it is easy and can be almost fatal when making choices entering in and going through retirement. Just like any good Sherpa, Abe has created a step by step guide to help you through what could otherwise be a dangerous journey, one false step or miscalculation can be disastrous. This book should become your guide to your retirement ascent. On a more personal note, having worked with Abe over the years, it has been such a rewarding experience watching him become one of the most successful and trusted advisors in the country. Abe—congratulations on this book. Continue to be the man and advisor you have become. Our industry and your clients are better for it."

> Michael Canet, JD, LLM
> Prostatis Financial

"As a dedicated retirement planner, *The Retirement Mountain* by Abe Abich stands out as a valuable guide for anyone preparing for retirement. Abich's metaphor of mountain climbing perfectly captures the challenges of both building and preserving wealth, no matter the number of zeros. His clear, actionable steps provide the clarity and confidence needed to navigate the complexities of retirement. I highly recommend this book for those who want to retire with added peace of mind and a well-structured plan."

> Jackie Campbell, CFP®, PFS, CPA
> CEO & Founder
> Campbell & Company

"Abe's passion for people and helping others navigate their retirement journey was evident throughout this book. As someone about to enter 'Phase 2' or the descent, I appreciate the comprehensive guide of things to consider, and I learned a lot. The questions throughout will be helpful conversation starters as my wife and I continue our planning."

> Jim Morgan
> C12 Chair

THE RETIREMENT MOUNTAIN™

THE 7 STEPS TO A LONG-LASTING RETIREMENT

ABE ABICH, CFF®

Copyright © 2024 Abe Abich, CFF®. All rights reserved.

The Retirement Mountain™: The 7 Steps to a Long-Lasting Retirement

No part of this book may be used or reproduced in any manner whatsoever without written permission of the publisher.

ISBN: 978-1-936961-22-1

Published by Wealth Advisor Books
Great Falls, VA 22066
www.wealthadvisorbooks.com

Printed in the United States of America

Disclosure
Abich Financial Wealth Management is a Registered Investment Advisor registered with the SEC. Registration as an investment adviser does not imply a certain level of skill or training, and the content of this communication has not been approved or verified by the United States Securities and Exchange Commission or by any state securities authority.

The information contained in this material is intended to provide general information about Abich Financial Wealth Management and its services. It is not intended to offer investment advice. Investment advice will only be given after a client engages our services by executing the appropriate investment services agreement. Information regarding investment products and services are provided solely to read about our investment philosophy and our strategies.

The content in this material is based on generally available information and is believed to be reliable. Abich Financial Wealth Management does not guarantee the accuracy of the information contained in this material.

Abich Financial Wealth Management will provide all prospective clients with a copy of our current Form ADV, Part 2A (Disclosure Brochure) prior to commencing an advisory relationship. However, at any time, you can view our current Form ADV, Part 2A at adviserinfo.sec.gov. In addition, you can contact us to request a hard copy.

Abich Financial Services, Inc. #127820 offers insurance products, including annuities, which are sold through licensed insurance agents of the firm. Insurance products and annuities are subject to the terms, conditions, and guarantees of the issuing insurance company. You should carefully consider your own insurance needs and financial objectives before purchasing insurance products.

DEDICATION

Mom and Dad, this book is dedicated to you. You are the ones who gave Josh and me inspiration, since we were young, to pursue our dreams. You were the ones who protected us, always supported us, believed in us, always encouraged us, constantly prayed for us, helped to keep us on the straight and narrow, and were always there for us in all we did and wanted to accomplish. You knew we could do anything we put our minds to.

Mom: you've always been my number one fan. You are a selfless saint. You are the G.O.A.T. The absolute best mother. I love you.

Dad: I know you are shining down from heaven watching over us. You would be so proud, I know it. I can still feel your love, your encouragement, your prayers. Your constant positivity and optimism. I love you.

It is with the utmost gratitude that I dedicate this book to you both. Thank you for all you did and continue to do for Josh and me and our families. I love you.

CONTENTS

Acknowledgements	vii
Foreword: My Passion for Helping Fellow Climbers	ix
Introduction: Climbing Your Retirement Mountain™	xiii

Part 1: The Ascent

Chapter 1:	Are You Ready to Climb Your Mountain?	3
Chapter 2:	Celebrating the Climb of Your Life	7
Chapter 3:	Retracing Your Steps	13
Chapter 4:	Why You May Need a Different Guide Coming Down the Mountain	21
Chapter 5:	Are You Ready to Retire?	23

Part 2: The View from the Summit

Chapter 6:	Soaking It All In	31
Chapter 7:	Imagining Your Next Life	35
Chapter 8:	Creating Your Future	39

Part 3: Possible Hazards as You Descend Your Retirement Mountain

Chapter 9:	The Sequence of Returns Hazard	47
Chapter 10:	Inflation Hazard	55

Part 4: The Descent—The Seven Steps Down the Retirement Mountain

Chapter 11:	Step 1—Develop a Retirement Income Plan and Roadmap	63
Chapter 12:	Step 2—A Road Map for Social Security	69
Chapter 13:	Step 3—Your Withdrawal and Distribution Plan	77
Chapter 14:	Step 4—Protect Your Life Savings	87
Chapter 15:	Step 5—Build a Tax Strategy	91
Chapter 16:	Step 6—Don't Forget Long-Term Care	97
Chapter 17:	Step 7—Plan for Your Legacy	103

Epilogue: Everyone Has an Everest	107
Appendix: Worksheet	110
About the Author	113

ACKNOWLEDGEMENTS

First, to my beautiful wife Shelly, thank you for inspiring me, for trusting me, for believing in me and our vision. For always being there for me. I'm a lucky man to be able to do life with you. I love you with all my heart.

To Josh, my best friend. I love you, brother. Thank you for your constant encouragement, belief in me and love. You are the best!

To Jason, my brother from another mother. Thank you for always being there for me. You are a selfless friend I can always count on. I love you, brother.

To Thomas Zebley, Evan Ward, Joel Tabin, Mike Canet, Chris Hoffman, Chris Hill, George Moore, Dave Borland, Jim Morgan, Stephen Odom. Thank you for your friendship, mentorship, and belief in me.

To Tim Fitzwilliams, Jeff Newell, Amir Asgharinejad, Pooyan Rahimi, Ryan Ferguson, Ryan Rauner, and any others I may have missed. Thank you for your friendships. They mean the world to me.

To Steve Eunpu, thank you for the vision you had for this book a long time ago. Thank you for your patience, wisdom, and pure determination to help me get this book finished.

To the rest of my family, thank you for always believing in me, encouraging me and loving me. I love you.

To my team at AFS. We've accomplished so much. We've helped so many families retire successfully. And we're just getting started. We have so much more work left to do. You are the best team in the industry. It's an honor and privilege to work together with you every day. Let's GO.

Finally, to my clients. You are why I get up every morning and come to work with passion, enthusiasm, and conviction. To help you, and many more, retire with dignity and confidence. Thank you for your business and trust in us. Thank you for your referrals to friends and family. It means the world to me and AFS.

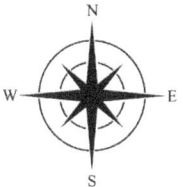

FOREWORD

MY PASSION FOR HELPING FELLOW CLIMBERS

I'm very fortunate that my career allows me to fulfill my personal calling and life mission: guiding people to develop the financial lives they deserve, so they can retire with dignity, confidence, and freedom from financial stress.

I never would have found this work without the inspiration of my parents. My father, Diego, arrived in the United States from Cuba in 1961. He had few dollars in his pocket but was motivated by a powerful hunger to live the American Dream.

My mother's name is Roberta, but she's Bobbe to everyone who knows her. She grew up in Hillside, NJ, where she met my father. The daughter of a nurse, all she knew was hard work and caring for her family, always focusing on others more than herself—the best mother that two boys could dream of having.

Dad believed education was extremely important to his success, so he constantly drove himself, pursuing opportunities to learn as he married, worked, and raised a family. He eventually earned two master's degrees and completed part of a Ph.D. Of course, he insisted I go to college and continue educating myself.

My father was a brilliant man, but one area of his education was lacking: how to manage and grow financial assets. That's why my parents always had meager savings and very little saved for their retirement.

I can't blame them. They did their best during lean years when each dollar was stretched to the maximum. Growing up with Joshua, my brother and best friend, we always had what we needed. But our family missed out on the American Dream of accumulating and growing wealth, not even owning a family home growing up.

Like many, my folks did their best, but they never received any education about money and finances. As a result, they made financial choices—such as renting a home year after year instead of buying—that would mean our family never generated many financial assets. We never went hungry (thanks to Mom clipping coupons out of the *Washington Post* every Sunday) or homeless. We got a new pair of shoes at the beginning of each new school year.

Most important, Joshua and I were raised in a strong, faith-filled Christian home where there was always more than enough love, support, and encouragement to go around. Our faith in God got us through everything; in a way, it was my parents' trust in Him that got us through those times.

MY CHANCE TO HELP OTHERS

When I launched my career at age twenty-three, I quickly realized that my parents weren't alone. Most people lack basic education in personal finances. Most people head into retirement unprepared. Too many begin climbing the Retirement Mountain too late. Sadly, few get the training and support they need to climb higher and safely descend the Retirement Mountain.

Addressing this knowledge deficit and lack of financial education has been my life's goal and mission ever since. Today, I have the privilege of working alongside my wife, who runs the company with me.

We're thrilled to have the support of an amazing team of passionate people, who work with us every day to achieve our shared educational mission. Working together for sixteen years, we've been able to help over a thousand families throughout the Northern Virginia and DC Metro area retire with dignity, confidence, and financial peace of mind.

Our number one goal is to prepare clients for a successful and long-lasting retirement. Preparing them means providing ongoing financial education so they can:

- Understand some of the complex issues involved in retirement planning; and

- Make sound financial decisions that will help them today and tomorrow.

THREE-PART PROCESS

First, we help people understand their **current situation**. Where are you today? Where do you stand today concerning your retirement? Have you saved enough? How close or far away are you?

Second, we help them discern where they want to be **tomorrow**. Where do you want to go?

Third, we help them weigh the pros and cons of the many options they face and make the best financial decisions for their unique desires and needs.

THE JOURNEY UPWARD

My job title may be "retirement planner," but my real-life mission is changing and improving people's lives.

I'm so grateful that my parents inspired me to discover this amazing calling, pursue it with all my heart, and serve the people who come to us day after day seeking guidance.

This work can be challenging, but it's incredibly rewarding, and I wouldn't have it any other way.

We would love to use our experience to help you climb your Retirement Mountain. Let's begin our journey.

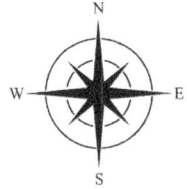

INTRODUCTION

CLIMBING YOUR RETIREMENT MOUNTAIN™

Retirement is a goal that people prepare for and look forward to for decades, patiently awaiting the day when they can say farewell to years of toil, saving, and planning. Many people believe they can finally relax and take it easy for a change once they've reached retirement age.

I wish this were the case, but navigating the ins and outs of retirement doesn't stop when you hit sixty-five or whatever your magic number is. In many ways, the day you retire is when you need to be most careful in your planning, thinking everything through, and making crucial decisions to protect and preserve the fruits of your labor.

This is why I often talk to clients about climbing the Retirement Mountain. As every experienced mountain climber knows, a climb includes two parts: the ascent and the descent.

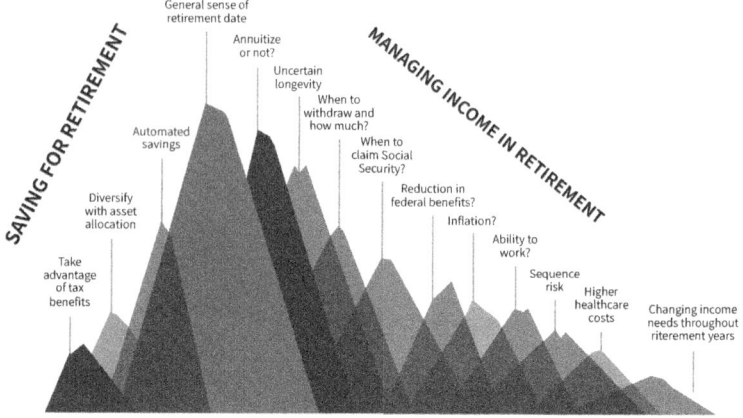

ON THE WAY UP

During the ascent, you are laser-focused on reaching the distant summit. As you climb upward, you try to avoid the loose boulders and potential spills that could prematurely end your adventure—and your life. If you're on a steep hike to higher elevations, you must pace yourself, ensuring you stay rested and hydrated.

At times, it looks like you're getting closer to the summit, but another vista opens up before you, revealing that your destination remains far away. Regardless, you do what you must: keep climbing, step after step, one foot in front of the other.

Once you've reached the summit, you can enjoy the amazing view, take a few photos. Then it's time to head back down.

ON THE WAY BACK DOWN

While it may seem counterintuitive to the novice, experienced mountain climbers know this truth: no matter how difficult, the ascent is the *easy* part of any climb.

It's on the descent that you will encounter the greatest risks and dangers. Amateurs may assume the descent is easier because you're no longer straining to gain elevation. But experienced mountain climbers know that 80 percent of mountaineering accidents happen on the way back down.

As you cautiously begin your descent down the mountain, you realize you're less energetic than you were on the way up, which is too bad because any missed step or misplaced rope could send you hurtling down, down, down to a serious injury or worse. Depending on the height of your mountain, you may experience freezing of your limbs or the "brain fog" accompanying the thin oxygen found at high altitudes.

Those who successfully make it safely back down can celebrate. They know they survived the lung-busting moments of the ascent, and then successfully avoided the worst dangers of the descent.

FROM MOUNTAINS TO MONEY: YOUR RETIREMENT JOURNEY

You can think of this book as a climber's guide. It's designed to help you travel your own Retirement Mountain. Let's further unpack our climbing metaphor so you can see what kind of journey is ahead of you.

CHALLENGES OF THE ASCENT

Likely, you're already familiar with the major challenges we confront on our climb up the mountain:

Your parents, upbringing, and your education. These all-important factors will influence everything that comes after.

Your career path. Will the income you generate during your career (the way up) be enough to take care of you during twenty to forty years of retirement (the way back down)?

Savings. Will you be able to put enough away for thousands of rainy days?

Wise investments. When your employer matches your 401(k) contributions, you ascend the mountain faster. It's the same when you take advantage of a health savings account, tax deferral, compound interest, and all the other important advantages that a good advisor can help you achieve.

Economic forces beyond your control. However well you practice and prepare for your climb, you never know when you will face a blinding blizzard or some other disaster. It's the same way with the potential challenges retirees face. You never know when something like the COVID pandemic will come along and knock you off your feet, forcing you to retrace your grueling steps.

DANGERS OF THE DESCENT

Reaching the summit is awesome. Finally freed from work demands, you can see the world around you from a new perspective.

But watch out. The climb back down poses dangers you didn't face on the way up. If you aren't properly prepared, everything you've worked for all these years may not get you as far as you'd hoped. These are some of your major dangers:

Income. First off, does your income exceed your expenses, inflation adjusted, for the rest of your life? Do you have multiple sources of income, and will you have enough for the long haul?

Earnings. Are your retirement savings achieving all they can? Are your investments properly diversified, helping you balance growth and risk while climbing back down?

Taxes. One of the biggest myths climbers on the way up tell themselves is that they will be in a lower tax bracket in retirement. Those making the descent know better. Taxes can eat into a wonderful accumulation plan.

Economic forces beyond your control. You faced this challenge on the way up. It can be even more dangerous on the way down. During the descent, make sure you watch out for inflation, which can shred your safety net.

This is just a preview of the adventure before you!

A CONFESSION

I want to acknowledge early on that my industry—the hundreds of thousands of people working in retirement and financial planning—have worked hard to help people climb the Retirement Mountain, getting TO the point of retirement. As a matter of fact, over 90 percent of our industry is what we call Phase 1, accumulation-based firms. You know the names of these firms, you see their commercials everywhere. This is not wrong or bad, it's great! However, with 10,000 baby boomers retiring daily for the next ten years in a row, and with less than 10 percent of our industry helping people in Phase 2, the income phase of retirement, there is a huge disconnect.

So, we've done a poor job, in my opinion, as an industry in helping people with the more dangerous part of their journey: their retirement years. In addition, just because a firm helped get you TO retirement doesn't mean they should be the firm helping you get THROUGH retirement. In most cases they should not be, as the focus is almost solely on pure accumulation.

I've seen the consequences of this failure too many times, so I've committed myself to guiding people on completing the whole journey, both finishing the ascent and getting down the descent safely.

Please put on your boots, grab some hiking poles, and let's go.

PART 1
THE ASCENT

For as long as there have been mountains, people have sought to climb them, often risking life and limb during grueling ascents and descents, all for that once-in-a-lifetime moment at the top that offers unparalleled views and rewards all the hard work.

Over time, climbing a mountain has become a metaphor for pretty much any challenge people seek to overcome.

In the 1965 movie *The Sound of Music*, the mountain metaphor becomes part of one of the most beautiful Rodgers & Hammerstein compositions, which features this memorable verse:

Climb every mountain,
Ford every stream,
Follow every rainbow,
'Till you find your dream.

The song expresses a wonderful sentiment, and it convinces Maria to "find the life you were born to live" by leaving the convent, where she was to become a nun, and marrying Captain von Trapp.

Unfortunately, there's one mountain that many people refuse to climb: the Retirement Mountain. They know they should do something about planning and preparing for retirement, but they ignore promptings, put it off, and hope things will take care of themselves.

But things don't always take care of themselves, and today millions of men and women are less prepared for retirement than their parents' generation was.

That's why you need this book. Let's get started.

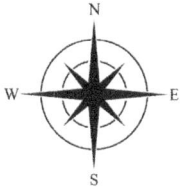

CHAPTER 1

ARE YOU READY TO CLIMB YOUR MOUNTAIN?

Randy wasn't sure where the idea came from, but before long it had grown into an overwhelming desire. He was going to climb a mountain.

Like many would-be adventurers, Randy had his heart set on something big. But when he started researching, he learned that climbing big mountains comes with big costs and risks. Climbing Mount Everest, the highest mountain on Earth, costs anywhere from $25,000 to $115,000, and ascending the main peak of Everest's Annapurna massif is risky, with a 29 percent fatality rate for climbers.

Randy reconsidered and started researching scalable mountains here in the states, coming up with a short list that included Camelback Mountain in Arizona, Mount Mansfield in Vermont, and California's Half Dome.

But before seriously considering climbing even one of these humbler mountains, Randy realized he needed to prepare, starting with getting himself into better physical shape. He started jogging, doing cardio exercises, and watching his diet.

Next, he started training his mind by taking classes, reading books, studying trail guides, and sharing tips with experienced hikers. He also found a guide, an experienced climber who would guide him during his early climbs, making sure he was following the proper protocols.

After months of planning, Randy was ready, organizing a trip to Arizona, where a guide would help him master Camelback Mountain.

YOUR RETIREMENT MOUNTAIN CALLS

Randy invested countless hours and thousands of dollars preparing himself for the physical challenge, but he overlooked less-exciting areas, completely ignoring information on how to climb Camelback Mountain.

He's not alone in skipping over the less-glamorous details and not being fully prepared. Americans facing retirement do the same thing. A 2018 *Wall Street Journal* headline warned: "Time Bomb Looms for Aging America: A Generation of Americans Is Entering Old Age the Least Prepared in Decades."

"Americans are reaching retirement age in worse financial shape than the prior generation, for the first time since Harry Truman was president," read the article. "More than 40 percent of households headed by people aged fifty-five through seventy lack sufficient resources to maintain their living standard in retirement. That is around fifteen million American households."

I've known many people like Randy. When they're consumed with an exciting challenge—mountain climbing, visiting Paris, driving across America in a big RV—they go at it with gusto.

But the more mundane concerns get less attention. The same thing happens with retirement readiness. In fact, most people spend more time planning their vacations than planning for retirement.

QUESTIONS ON THE ASCENT

Once people start working and earning money, they are already climbing the Retirement Mountain, whether or not they realize it. Those who know it and plan accordingly usually achieve greater success in their climb. At the same time, those who ignore all the boring but important details about investment portfolios, risk, asset allocation, and rates of return may face a financial avalanche.

Retirement advisors can serve as expert guides for those climbing the Retirement Mountain. When we work with people to prepare them for the journey ahead, we're often asked questions like these:

- Will I earn enough and save enough to last me throughout my retirement life?

- How long will I need to work?

- What impact will financial forces like inflation have on my life in retirement?

- How do I control the amount of taxes I pay?

- How do I maximize my Social Security benefits and retirement income?

- How do I manage risk and achieve retirement security?

- What about health? How do I prepare for the increased expenses of long-term healthcare?

- Will I have enough to provide for my wife/husband and children/grandchildren when I die?

- What will I be able to give to charities that support my values?

EVERY CLIMB TAKES PREPARATION

The planning and preparation Randy invested in helped his initial mountain climb go well, and he has since sought other opportunities to scale higher peaks.

If he could invest similar energy in planning for his future, the payoffs would be well worth the investment.

As he faces the journey ahead, he needs to honestly consider his desires for the future, face his uncertainty and fears about reaching his goals, confront problems, and ask hard questions about how he wants to live his life. His lifestyle plan will be just as important as his retirement plan.

There are many similarities between mountain climbing and the Retirement Mountain:

- When are you planning to finish your climb up and start your descent down the mountain?

- How high do you want to climb? How much money do you want and need to save to accomplish a wonderful descent?

- How much risk are you willing to face along the way?

- How prepared are you for the challenges to come and all of the risks that can mess up a fantastic savings plan?

Let's take a closer look at these questions as we help you prepare for your climb.

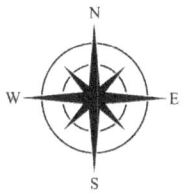

CHAPTER 2

CELEBRATING THE CLIMB OF YOUR LIFE

In retirement, you face a dangerous descent full of new challenges that will test all your training. We will get you fully prepared for that in the next chapter. But before we start that arduous journey down the mountain, I want you to slow down and enjoy the view.

There's nothing like the 360-degree view from a mountaintop, so stop, take a few deep breaths, look all around you, and for a few moments appreciate and be thankful for everything you've done in life and all these steps you took to bring you to this moment.

Life presents each of us with life-changing decisions and life-threatening encounters, but somehow, you've made it through. You've not only survived; in many ways, you've thrived!

LANDMARKS PASSED

Before you start the next stage of your journey, look back at the amazing trek you've already completed and the seven major landmarks you've passed along the way.

You survived birth. Congratulations! You've made it this far, even though the odds of being born were infinitesimally small: one in 102,685,000—that's right, a 10 followed by 2,685,000 zeroes, according to one researcher.

First, there was a one in 20,000 chance that your mother and father would meet. The chances of them marrying were better than that, but the odds of staying together long enough to produce a child—you!—was one in 2,000.

The challenges don't stop once you're born. In your first year of life, your likelihood of dying is incredibly low: 0.006081, or six-tenth of a percentage point. But year by year, the possibility increases. By age eighty-five, your death probability rate rises to 0.095062, or 9.5 percent chance of dying in a year.

Too many people take life itself for granted. Don't let that happen to you. You've survived to a ripe old age. Say three cheers for yourself!

You made it through high school. There were perhaps hundreds of mornings when you wanted to do anything else but get up, get dressed, and go to school. But you listened to the advice of your nagging parents and did it anyway, day after day, grade after grade.

Finally, you graduated, which about 85 percent of public high school students eventually do.

You may not have your paper diploma any longer, but you have enjoyed the benefits it conferred. Not only did you learn many things, but you also prepared the way for a better future.

You worked a part-time job. In high school, you may have been a lifeguard, a burger flipper, a retail clerk, or a professional landscape artist (a.k.a., mower of lawns.)

Whatever it was, you got a summer job, learned how to do it, and did it well enough not to get fired and get paid, just like 17 percent of teens aged sixteen to nineteen.

If you were especially hard-working, or if your family was poor and needed your additional income, you worked throughout the school year, too.

Learning to keep a job, make money, and earn promotions are valuable life skills. Thankfully, you developed these skills somewhere along the way and used them for the rest of your life.

All these years later, your hard work has paid off.

You learned to manage money. Like all of us, you wasted at least a portion of your meager wages on momentary pleasures and silly purchases you may have later regretted. But in time, you developed the ability to defer gratification, which kept your spending in check and even allowed you to save a little bit.

Most young people aren't so savvy. A third of American teenagers don't have bank accounts, and about half rely on mobile or online apps to manage their financial lives.

Teens under eighteen can't apply for a credit card without Mom or Dad cosigning. But somehow, 50 percent of incoming first-year college students already carry credit-card debt averaging $1,585. By sophomore year, 92 percent of students have at least one credit card.

Young people face tremendous financial pressure, but you resisted most of the worst temptations, which has contributed to where you are today.

You continued schooling after high school. For about 45 percent of young men, high school is the end of their formal education.

For young women, the rate is lower: about 30 percent of female high school graduates don't attend college.

Today, about 38 percent of Americans twenty-five years or older have a bachelor's degree from a four-year institution, and 14 percent have advanced graduate or professional degrees. A little over 10 percent have an associate degree from a two-year institution. And about 15 percent start but do not finish college.

College is intellectually demanding and expensive, and many families can't afford it, causing some students to go into debt. But you invested in a degree because you thought it would pay off later in life, and it has.

You chose a good major. You could have filled your college class schedule with physical education classes, music appreciation courses, or easy offerings such as those that are offered at major universities: "geology and cinema," "sport for the spectator," or "Lady Gaga and the sociology of fame."

But those weren't the courses you took. You chose a demanding major that promised you a lucrative career after college, and you took all the courses required for that major, even if you didn't like them all or had to repeat a class or two.

You worked hard in your career or trade. Your education was over; you made your way in the world of work. But thanks to that education, you did better than some other folks.

Employment rates vary according to how much education a person has:

- Eighty-six percent of twenty-five to thirty-four year olds with a bachelor's or higher degree were employed as of 2020.

- The employment rate for those who started but did not finish college was 78 percent.

- For those with only a high school diploma, 69 percent were employed.

- Only 57 percent of those who didn't complete high school were employed.

AN ATTITUDE OF GRATITUDE

Enjoy the view. You've had a long journey full of many unexpected twists and turns, but you hung in there, persevered, and successfully made it through adulthood.

Take a moment to appreciate all the good things that have happened to you and how your hard work has generated significant rewards. And don't forget to thank the adults who served as role models and mentors, helping you make important decisions. You couldn't have done it without them.

Now, we will focus on how you can apply the skills and lessons you've learned so far for your descent down the Retirement Mountain.

CHAPTER 3

RETRACING YOUR STEPS

They call it "Everesting," but instead of traveling to Nepal and spending tens of thousands of dollars and a few months trying to climb the actual Mt. Everest, participants climb 29,029 feet—the height of Everest—in installments on smaller mountains elsewhere.

I signed up with several financial advisor and industry friends to climb 29,029 feet in the Wasatch Mountains of Utah, Snowbasin, in August 2022. Months ahead, we started our preparation by doing regular workouts and conditioning that strengthened our bodies and minds for the journey ahead. We had thirty-six hours to complete this mission, from Friday morning at 6 a.m. to Saturday at 6 p.m. If you complete thirteen ascents up Snowbasin, 2,310 feet per ascent, after thirteen ascents and nearly thirty miles later, you would have climbed 29,029 feet. And we did. And it was the hardest thing I've ever done in my life up to that point, both physically and mentally.

The weather in Utah is better than Everest, where lack of oxygen, frigid temperatures, and sudden storms threaten even the most experienced climbers. And instead of taking days to reach the summit and sleeping on a frigid mountainside in a sleeping bag, we returned to our hotel the next day so we could shower, eat a nice meal, and sleep in a comfortable bed.

Still, the climb remained a major challenge as we made progress hourly until we had accomplished the task of climbing more than thirty miles in vertical elevation.

Reflecting on the experience later, I realized that our experience in Utah was similar to what most people experience day after day. Instead of making a straight beeline up the mountain of life, most of us climb in stages, experiencing small victories and occasional defeats along the way as we confront each new challenge we face as we continue our ascent. One foot in front of the other, day by day, progress is made. It's the consistent daily actions that add up to be so much years later.

Progress in life—and in retirement—is often made in installments. We take two steps forward; then, we must take a step or two back as we continue our ascent.

A FEW STEPS FORWARD...

From your perspective on the mountaintop, you can see how far you've climbed as you progress, step-by-step.

Remember when you landed your **first full-time job**? Suddenly, you had a position with a title, a desk (and, if fortunate, your own office), and maybe even a business card that spelled out who you were now.

In a couple weeks, you received your reward: **your first paycheck**. I still remember how I felt holding my first check and looking at the numbers inscribed. What a thrill it was to to get paid for hard work.

I also remember looking at the numbers on my pay stub. **Payroll taxes and contributions to Social Security** were deducted from my check and reduced my take-home pay. I had conflicting feelings. I was a little miffed that the money I earned wasn't going to me, but it also felt good to know I was investing in my future, which at that point seemed a long way off. In your twenties, thinking about your fifties and sixties seems like a world away.

. . . AND ONE STEP BACK

With my increased earning power, I received regular solicitations from credit card companies inviting me to **sign up for credit cards** and experience the good life that would come through my many member benefits.

Thankfully, I did better than some in disciplining myself in using credit, but not all take this approach. Many wind up charging themselves into debt, slowing or even halting their climb up the mountain and eventually forcing them to pay up for past purchases.

FROM "ME" TO "US"

As you continue your journey through life, you make friends, including one special friend you decide you wanted to spend the rest of your life with. You may have been in love before, but **marriage** takes things to a whole new level.

You survive the challenges of wedding planning, enjoy a brief honeymoon, and then return to the **apartment or or perhaps your first house** that the two of you will call home as you fill it with furnishings.

Before long, a third member of the family is sometimes on the way, perhaps a pet or your first child, along with a host of changes in how both of you will spend your time and money.

IN THE ZONE

You work diligently, traveling nonstop, turning in long hours, and earning promotions and raises. You are determined to make your money work smart, both now and in the future, and that inspires you to make a few smart moves.

Curious about your workplace benefits, you meet with Human Resources and sign up for everything you think will help, including:

- Enrolling in your employer's 401(k) plan (naturally, you take advantage of company matching, which effectively increases your contribution);

- Opting for a higher level of care on the company's health and dental plans;

- Purchasing life insurance;

- And contributing to a health savings account (HSA).

You know these important steps will pay off in the future.

FAMILY AND FINANCES

Your family continues to grow and, as it does, you soon realize that your existing home and automobiles aren't big enough to handle everyone.

You feel some nagging uncertainty as you sign up for a new car loan and apply for a mortgage on a bigger house, but you are confident your growing income will cover your increasing expenses.

Everything is more expensive now. The two of you could take a quick weekend getaway cheaply, but now, family vacations are more complex and costly.

Parenting Is Costly

The average cost of raising a child born to a middle-income, married couple is approximately $267,000 (in 2021 dollars) over eighteen years—or more than $14,800 a year per child for a typical two-child household, according to *U.S. News & World Report*.

SEEKING ADVICE

As growing sums of money flow into and out of the family piggy bank, you make a wise decision. You contact a financial advisor (or wealth advisor), who works with you to determine how to maximize your income and savings to accumulate the maximum possible assets during this phase of your life so you can prepare for the next phases.

Your financial choices and decisions now determine how high you will ascend in the future. Your planning and actions determine how much you have in your 401(k), savings, and equity in your house.

Over time, your assets grow and, before you know it, you have amassed $500,000, one million, or more in assets. You realize that these assets must last the rest of your life, and the more you have at your disposal, the better things will be.

Life looks good.

A WORD FROM MOTHER NATURE

The meteorologists called it a hundred-year storm, but all you know is that a raging torrent of muddy water tore through your backyard late one night, transporting a wet mess into your carpeted basement. Some $20,000 later, everything is mostly back to normal.

> ### OBSTACLES ON THE MOUNTAIN— A BROKEN HOME
>
> Maybe it was the growing work travel and continuing long hours. Perhaps it was increased tensions caused by differences in parenting techniques. Whatever the cause, for some, a rift started between your partner and you and continued growing. Unfortunately, everyone was too busy to attend to the widening gulf until, suddenly, everything broke apart.
>
> "I want a divorce."
>
> Two people who were bound in love now split up amid tension and animosity, and along with all the emotional pain comes a heavy dose of economic distress. Now there are two households to fund, significantly slowing your progress up the mountain.

BIG-TICKET ITEMS

As your kids get older, their expenses grow, particularly as they approach two major life decisions.

- Paying for college. The costs vary widely from state to state and depend on whether your kids will attend public or private schools. Public schools cost around $11,000 per year for in-state tuition, while in-state tuition for private schools average around $40,000 annually.

- Paying for weddings. The national average wedding cost is just over $20,000, but many spend much more.

Your financial advisor helps you figure out what you can afford.

Meanwhile, your parents are getting older and, like many in their generation, they aren't prepared financially for the higher costs of healthcare and the need for long-term housing as more and more people live into their eighties and nineties.

LOOKING AHEAD

As you near the end of your working and earning years, you want to ensure your future is secure, so you call an advisor to analyze your asset allocations and expenses.

Based on projections for the next two decades, your advisor tells you to diversify your assets to protect you from economic uncertainties.

"This is what you will need for the long haul."

Two Kinds of Advisors

Anyone can claim to be a financial advisor, but only some possess the training, experience, and certifications necessary to provide the best advice.

Throughout your life, you will likely need two kinds of advisors: one for the ascent and another for the descent. These advisors are like your financial sherpas, assisting you in your climb up and down the mountain.

- Phase 1, ascent advisors: During the upward climb, traditional wealth advisors focus on maximizing assets.

- Phase 2, descent advisors: But during your climb down the Retirement Mountain, you need different help. In our work with clients, we guide them on the descent down the mountain, making sure their assets are properly put to work so they can last for the long haul.

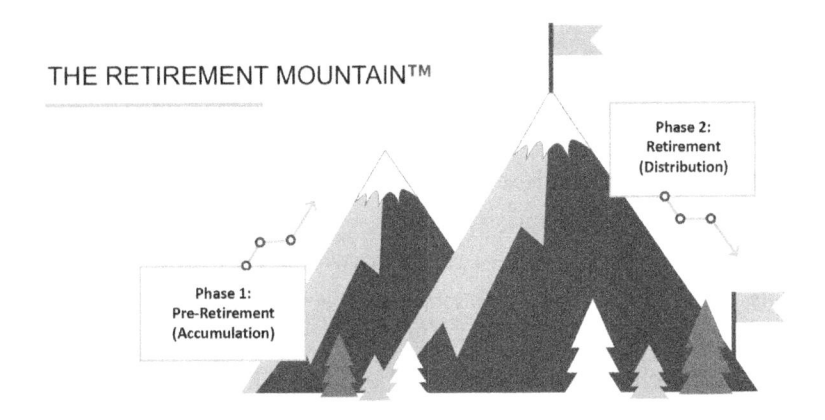

THE RETIREMENT MOUNTAIN™

Phase 2: Retirement (Distribution)

Phase 1: Pre-Retirement (Accumulation)

NEW PERILS AHEAD

What a long and winding journey you have taken, with thrilling victories and shocking upsets.

Thankfully, you've made it this far in relatively good shape, but this is no time to forget the task ahead. The challenges coming in the next few decades will play a major role in your descent down the Retirement Mountain.

CHAPTER 4

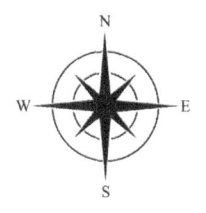

WHY YOU MAY NEED A DIFFERENT GUIDE COMING DOWN THE MOUNTAIN

Mountain climbing brings different kinds of pain.

When climbing up a mountain, you usually feel it first in your calves, hamstrings, and glutes. No matter how much training you've done, most are surprised by how worn out their legs are when they reach the top.

When coming back down, it's a whole different story. It's much harder on your knees and quads.

During the ascent, your leg muscles strain to elevate your body step-by-step up the mountain.

During the descent, gravity pulls you downward and your legs act like brakes to slow your speed. With each downward step, the entire weight of your body and everything you carry with you is pressing down, first on one knee and then another, compressing your knee joints and creating a lot of pressure in the front part of your legs.

It's all the same mountain, but the challenges you face going up are different than those you face going down.

Good training and experience can help climbers deal with the perils they face along the way: dehydration and lack of nutrition, not to mention the intense mental stress. Likewise, a trained financial sherpa can help you climb your Retirement Mountain.

TWO DIFFERENT KINDS OF CHALLENGES

It's the same with retirement, as mentioned in the previous chapter. During the ascent, it's all about accumulating and maximizing your assets. Step-by-step, you're straining to earn more and save more. The focus is building and accumulating the resources you will need later.

Many wealth advisors can help you during the ascent, and as long as you still have income, pretty much whatever they do looks like it's working.

But once you start the descent, and your previous sources of income may slow or stop, you need a different kind of help to meet these additional challenges.

As you prepare to head back down the mountain, you must do everything you can to resist the financial forces of gravity that want to deplete the resources you've spent your life working to acquire.

You must realize that the people who helped you during the ascent may not offer the best guidance during the descent.

Let's take a look at the key issues a good advisor will want to explore with you.

CHAPTER 5

ARE YOU READY TO RETIRE?

When you're climbing a mountain, there are times when it looks like you're just about to reach the top, but once you realize there are more switchbacks as you continue your climb to the top, the peak remains far off.

What about retirement? When do you know when you've reached the top of your Retirement Mountain and are ready to start the trek back down?

A good financial advisor who knows the way around mountains of various shapes and sizes can give you essential guidance and let you know if your climb is over or you still have a way to go.

CHECKING YOUR EQUIPMENT

It's been a long climb so far, but it's not over yet. Time for a checkup:

How are your hiking shoes holding up?

How are you doing physically and mentally?

How is your nutrition and hydration?

How about your gear? Are you paying attention to the weather and what you may need, whether it's hot or cold?

Even though you're drained, do you have what it takes to finish your climb?

It's the same with retirement. A qualified advisor can help determine if you are truly equipped to retire. Here's a checklist of the six things you need to make retirement work for you.

1. YOUR INVESTMENTS

You have spent decades building your retirement portfolio. Now it's time to see what you've got and how much it's worth.

- Start with 401(k)s, 403(b)s, or Thrift Savings Plans if you are a government employee or in the military.

- Include any IRAs, traditional or Roth, SEP, and SIMPLEs.

- Include any brokerage accounts, trust accounts, gold, and silver.

- And don't forget cash, CDs, savings bonds, and other liquid assets you own.

Once you tally up all these investments, you will be in much better shape to figure out whether you can retire now or should wait until later.

2. YOUR PROPERTY

What do you own, and how much is it worth? Creating a detailed inventory of all your property is an essential preparation step.

- Start with your primary residence, which, for many Americans, is their biggest asset. What is your house value, the loan amount, and how much principle and interest must you pay in the coming years?

- Then add other real estate holdings, again including loan amounts and what is left to be paid off.

- Finally, factor in other personal property, including cars, boats, recreational vehicles, jewelry, and other valuables.

3. INCOME SOURCES

- Social Security

- Pensions

- Rental Income

- Deferred Compensation

4. YOUR EXPENSES

It's great tallying up everything on the plus side of the ledger. Now it's time to look at the cost side and determine how much you spend daily.

- Start with fixed expenses: the bills you must pay month after month.

- Remember to include your spending for entertainment, meals out, and other discretionary expenditures.

- Finally, factor in how much you spend every year on vacations.

5. INSURANCE POLICIES

- Long-Term Care Insurance

Do you have long-term care insurance?

If you do, calculate your daily benefit, the time these benefits last, the policy issue date, and whether your policy includes an inflation rider.

If you don't have long-term care insurance, have you considered it and investigated the potential costs and benefits?

- Life Insurance

If you carry life insurance, your advisor will want to know the company, the type of insurance you have, if your policy has cash value, and the premiums.

6. YOUR ESTATE PLANNING

- Wills and Trusts

Do you have a will or trust?

If so, when was your will or trust last updated?

If you don't have a will, advanced medical directives, or power of attorney, have you considered them and learned about the pros and cons?

After working for decades, many people can begin retirement as soon as possible. Once you have calculated what you have in these six key categories, you'll better understand how prepared you are for your retirement future.

Note: See the Appendix at the back of the book for a summary worksheet.

PART 2

THE VIEW FROM THE SUMMIT

The journey was both exhausting and thrilling. You've seen amazing sights you never imagined before. You have experienced challenges you never anticipated but eventually overcame. Different parts of your body have experienced pains you've never faced before.

All in all, it's been quite a climb!

You can't hang around at the summit forever. Your stay here on top of the world must be brief. But before you head back down, take a moment to enjoy the unparalleled panorama. No other place on Earth offers such a perspective.

While you're looking around, thank your lucky stars. Not everyone who starts climbing a mountain will reach the top. Some four thousand brave souls have summitted Mt. Everest. At least two thousand have tried but failed. At least three hundred have died trying.

I don't want to ruin your fun, but it's worth noting that the descent is more dangerous than the ascent. Deadly falls and bodily collapse are more common on returning to the base of the mountain, partly because your body is exhausted, and your mind can be clouded by high-altitude brain fog. But don't worry too much. The expert guides can help take you back down.

Enjoy the view for a bit more. You've earned it. Then, as soon as you think you're ready, start focusing your mind on your next journey: the climb back down.

CHAPTER 6

SOAKING IT ALL IN

After a freezing-cold climb that threatened to turn your feet, hands, and everything else into a big human ice cube, there's nothing like getting down off the mountain, stripping off the bulky clothing that protected you from the cold, and stepping into a nice, big hot tub. As the bubbles circle your aching body, the pains seem to disappear on the clouds of steam.

You may have similar feelings when you reach the top of your Retirement Mountain. You started your climb decades ago, and you kept at it workday after workday, month after month, year after year, doing everything you could to prepare for this moment.

Relief is one of the emotions that many people feel at this important juncture in life. Sudden freedom from the relentless schedules and demands of work can be intoxicating. Make sure you enjoy it. Soak it in.

Unfortunately, reaching the top of your Retirement Mountain isn't as dramatic or newsworthy as summiting Everest. Millions retire yearly, so no one is there to photograph your final step. Your hometown newspaper isn't going to celebrate you as an heroic athlete. It's up to you to celebrate as you see fit.

Many people celebrate this important milestone by hosting retirement parties, often organized as a surprise by family members and professional peers who love you and honor your work.

Enjoy these gatherings and the greeting cards and gag gifts people give you. These celebrations and displays of support will provide you with many warm memories you can cherish in the years ahead.

Many people celebrate retirement by finally taking that big overseas trip they've been looking forward to for years. Whether it's a golf and whiskey tour of Scotland, a trip to visit the ancient remains of Peru's Machu Picchu, or a bit of volcano tourism to one of the world's fifteen hundred active volcanoes, nothing says retirement quite like taking a nice long trip during which you can ignore your wristwatch and cell phone if you like, because nobody from work is looking for you any longer.

Some people celebrate retirement closer to home by exchanging their old work uniform for more comfortable clothing and adopting a daily schedule that they can dictate rather than answering to someone else's plan. Some may find their life busier than when they worked full-time.

Others celebrate by investing more time and energy in relationships that were difficult to maintain during the busy, go-go years of family and career. Now that your time is your own, you can invest more in the people you love.

Inevitably, some celebrations will be accompanied by feelings of dislocation as you find your way in your new life, grief as you miss the people and activities work once provided you, or even anxiety as you worry about whether or not you are as prepared for retirement as you thought.

Your Phase 2 fiduciary retirement planner can help you address these concerns in due time, but don't let these worries cloud your celebration. You have surpassed a monumental milestone. Make sure you pat yourself on the back and congratulate yourself on a job well done and all the preparations you have made for the future.

CHAPTER 7

IMAGINING YOUR NEXT LIFE

About half of the people our firm advises enter retirement having already planned out what they hope to do during this new chapter of life, while the other half hasn't figured that out yet.

Whether we're working with the decided or the undecided, one of our favorite things is encouraging people to imagine their possible retirement futures by asking them about their bucket lists.

Some respond quickly, while others need to think about it.

We get it. Many people have no idea what to expect or what they want to experience. That's not surprising, because the realities of retirement are so new and alien to them. They know what their old life was like: long hours, hectic commutes, difficult assignments, and all of it rewarded with a regular paycheck. Now that all these things are gone, some people are lost and uncertain about what to do next.

There's a term to describe this existential uncertainty: failure of imagination. Parents raising kids encourage their children to imagine all they can be and go for it with gusto. Now that the kids are gone, it's time for Mom and Dad to do some imagining of their own.

These questions may help you imagine your possible futures:

What makes you happy?

What tasks have you always dreamed of accomplishing?

What adventures have you imagined exploring?

Where have you always wanted to travel? America's national parks? Australia's vast deserts?

What hobbies and skills have you longed to develop more fully?

Which friends, families, and loved ones do you want to spend more time with?

What community groups have you considered helping and supporting with your time and resources?

What books have you desired to read that you haven't been able to yet?

What kinds of special things could you do with your grandkids?

How can you deepen your faith journey?

Failure to answer these questions will result in opportunities missed, horizons lowered, and joy that remains unexperienced.

I suspect that most people who successfully make it up and back down Mount Everest don't immediately start planning their next mountain trek within twenty-four hours. But after some rest and recovery, many start focusing on their next challenge.

What mountain will you climb next? What challenges are you desiring to take on? What social problems are you hoping to improve?

Decades ago, you probably asked yourself what you wanted to be growing up. Now that you're all grown up, it's time to answer that question again.

What do you want to do with the rest of your life? Start by imagining the possibilities. The lifestyle plan you create now will be just as important as your Phase 2 retirement plan.

CHAPTER 8

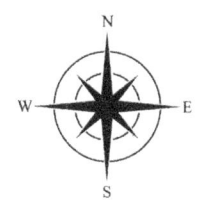

CREATING YOUR FUTURE

Your working life probably involved plenty of important choices and decisions. Now get ready for the host of questions you must confront in retirement!

Do you want to downsize? Or should you finally add that backyard swimming pool? Or buy that beautiful vacation home on the lake?

Should you buy a motorcycle, a boat, or splurge on a motor home?

Are you saying a final farewell to work and career, or should you continue working part-time or consulting?

Do you want to plant a new vegetable garden, or do you want to spend the summer traveling the world?

Do you want to put something away for the grandkids' college funds?

MAKING YOUR DREAMS CONCRETE

In the previous chapter, you imagined the possible retirement futures you would like to live. In this chapter, we show you how to convert these desires into concrete choices so you can create that future for yourself and loved ones.

Underneath the many questions retirement brings, there's one major question you must address: *How in the world are we going to pay for all of this?*

This question helps put all the others in context, and we will address it more fully in Part 4.

Previously, your choices about what to do were restricted by your commitments to children, work, and other obligations. What do you want to do now that you are freed from some of these demands?

RECONSIDERING YOUR PRIORITIES

You are not alone if you find it difficult to answer some of these questions. If you're stuck, I recommend revisiting the questions in the previous chapter and revising your three chosen priorities. Also, figure out which of these three to put first; for example, some retirees focus on travel while they have the physical stamina to do it.

Hardly anybody can do everything they dream of doing. The limitations of time, energy, and money have a way of helping people narrow things down and sort things out.

But don't let these limitations put a damper on your dreams. Dream big to start and, if necessary, curtail your ambitions if they threaten your overall plans.

THE "WHERE" QUESTION

Once you've figured out *what* you want to do, the next big question you will face in retirement is *where* will you do it?

For years, your housing choices were limited by your work location and family members. Now that you're free from many of your old duties and responsibilities, where do you want to live? The choices are endless.

Do we keep our current house or sell it and move somewhere else?

How much of our old stuff do we need and want to keep?

What kind of new living space do we want?

Do we want to move where we can be closer to kids and grandkids?

Do we want to move into a retirement community, like Jimmy Buffet's Margaritaville, based on his hit song, or something more settled from an earlier generation of retirement living, like Sun City, Arizona?

Do we go south for sun and surf? Or do we want to avoid hurricanes and rising sea levels and hunker down in Scottsdale, Boise, or Denver? (Before Hurricane Ian hit Florida in 2022, Fort Myers Beach was the sixth fastest-growing area in the U.S.)

With our medical challenges, should we live near our doctors' offices?

Or do we want to get out of Dodge, get off the grid, and leave it all behind?

THE "WHERE" QUESTION'S BIG IMPACT

Deciding where to live seems like it should be a simple question, but it is often one of the most complex and consequential decisions retirees make. Where you live has a major impact on your social and financial future.

Some completely ditch the idea of having a permanent residence or address and instead sell the house, buy a motorhome or recreational vehicle, and spend their next life stage migrating from place to place.

Some buy a tiny house with two-hundred to six-hundred square feet of living space and plant it in their kid's backyard.

For some people, the answers come down to finances. That's why many Americans have decided they should spend their retirement years in Mexico, Central or Latin America, or southeast Asia, which can be much more affordable than living in most American cities.

HELP NEEDED

Many people who expect the "where" question to be simple grow frustrated when they realize how complex and impactful this question can be. And when you answer one question, it seems like that choice limits your options on other questions.

These are the moments when many people say, "You know what? I could use some expert guidance in figuring all of this out."

Thankfully, there's nothing we like more than providing that guidance to people through each and every one of the many retirement decisions they must make. We can help you see how your choices in one area may significantly impact your choices in other areas.

FINE-TUNING YOUR PLAN

The "where" question is just one of numerous choices you must make, each of them full of significant consequences. Here are some of the questions we would like to help you navigate:

Can you afford to retire now?

If so, what kind of retirement can you afford?

What should you do with your resources: protect them or grow them? Both?

Should you start taking Social Security as soon as you hit retirement age, or wait a few years longer?

What does the math say?

Should you sell your home and rent?

Do you take out a construction loan to add a new sunroom or use funds from your 401(k)?

Which states have the lowest cost of living? Which are most tax-friendly?

You're worried because you see stories about declines in the stock market. What should you do to protect your retirement nest egg?

THE "HOW" QUESTION

Sooner or later, questions about retirement become questions about how to afford retirement. That's why we are here, to help people turn their dreams into reality. Sometimes, that means a reality adjustment that ensures the goals are attainable. In other cases, people need to dream bigger, assured that their resources truly allow them to do whatever they want.

We love helping people articulate their dreams for the future and and helping them do everything they can to realize them. There's nothing like being able to tell someone who's anxious and worried that they're OK, that they will be able to achieve many of their dreams.

We help people turn dreams into plans and then put those plans into action.

Let's take a closer look at some of the hazards you may face as you descend your Retirement Mountain.

PART 3

POSSIBLE HAZARDS AS YOU DESCEND YOUR RETIREMENT MOUNTAIN

After decades of working, saving, and investing, you have reached the top of the Retirement Mountain. You've enjoyed your time at the top and your panoramic view of the world. Now it's time to prepare for making your descent down the mountain and into full-time retirement living.

But your journey back down the mountain won't be the same as your journey up. You are a different person now than when you started your career, and your financial situation is very different.

The top of the mountain is a transition zone between your climb and your descent, and there are seven essential steps you need to carefully map out as you journey into your retirement future.

As you descend your Retirement Mountain, be aware that there will be challenges and hazards that you will face.

CHAPTER 9

THE SEQUENCE OF RETURNS HAZARD

Ruth Woroniecki had a plan for Christmas Eve in 2022. She would hike up Mount Baldy in California's San Gabriel Mountains early in the morning and then be back down before dinner.

Her ascent up the mountain went great, but the descent didn't go well.

The forty-year-old woman from Colorado slipped on some ice on her way back down, then fell two hundred feet down the side of the mountain, sliding and bouncing until she ran into a tree head-first, which stopped her fall but caused significant cuts on her head and left her unconscious in the cold.

A rescue helicopter found her and lowered an emergency worker to a nearby site. The worker hiked to her location and moved her to a more accessible area where the helicopter could rescue her and fly her to a hospital.

"She required dozens of stitches and staples to close the laceration in her head," said a San Bernardino County sheriff, "and neural surgery to repair the damage to her spine. She has a long road ahead of therapy and treatment."

Similar dangers await on the Retirement Mountain, as shown in this book. People climbing the Retirement Mountain can't wait to get to the top and start putting their retirement dreams into motion.

But then, if something unexpected happens, they may slip and slide as they head into retirement, like one couple we know.

MARKET MAYHEM

Bill and Anne came to our office for guidance. The couple was in their mid-sixties and had worked and saved all their lives, but they hadn't done much real planning. They came to see us because they wanted to retire by the end of the year.

But just as they firmed up their plans, changes in financial markets hammered their savings. They had saved up $1.5 million but lost $275,000 due to a combination of brutal factors. A forty-year-high inflation rate caused by quantitative easing, federal stimulus packages, corporate bailouts, lowered interest rates, and increased market volatility caused markets to sink nearly 20 percent.

In a seeming blink of an eye, the money they had worked years to earn evaporated. If this loss had happened years earlier, they might have been able to make up for it, but it instead came just as they were planning to quit working and live on savings.

Timing may not be everything, but it's one of many important factors. In the world of retirement investing, we call this challenge the "sequence of returns."

DEFINING THE CULPRIT

Called sequence risk or sequence of returns risk, this is the danger retirees face when withdrawing from their retirement accounts.

If the markets are down at the same time you make withdrawals, you get the double whammy of a double negative (your withdrawal plus the market loss).

You might think, "I would never withdraw money when the markets are down." But it happens to people all the time once they hit age seventy-three and experience required minimum distributions RMDs).

If sequence risk happens early in the retirement distribution years, it can be terminal for your life savings and portfolio. Many retirees don't have the three-to-five years typically needed to recover from a -20 percent or greater loss.

You can eliminate sequence risk by having dollars set aside that don't participate in market downturns, i.e., principal-protected instruments. You can also minimize sequence risk by reducing volatility in your portfolio.

You can win by not losing in retirement and you can certainly win in retirement by avoiding large losses. Avoiding large losses may perhaps be the number-one thing a retiree can do to secure their retirement.

UNDERSTANDING THE SEQUENCE OF RETURNS

Bill and Anne took a major financial hit as they were ready to stop working and descend the Retirement Mountain. Their near 20 percent loss of portfolio value punched a hole in some of their dreams.

This is a classic example of how the order and timing of poor investment returns can greatly impact how long your retirement savings last.

Other people retire when markets are climbing, and their retirement savings swell. That's good for them.

Markets can be unpredictable. Suppose your retirement savings undergo a loss while you start to withdraw your savings for living expenses. In that case, this can significantly impact your portfolio's overall value, meaning you risk running out of money before you planned.

This happened to millions during the Lost Decade of 2000–2012. Let's take a look at this terrible time in the markets and the S&P 500 specifically.

THE LOST DECADE

Between the years 2000 and 2012 the S&P 500 was negative.

For example: If you invested $1 million in the S&P 500 in the year 2000, you would only have about $935,000 by year 2012.

How can that happen? For starters, we had the tech bubble and September 11th in the years 2000, 2001, and 2002. The S&P 500 lost about 46 percent during these three years. It took five great years to recover those losses. Then 2008 hit: -38%. Another four years from 2009 to 2012 to recover from that massive loss. Finally, one would have been positive in 2013.

No decade had been so bad for investors since the years following the Great Depression. This time, a housing collapse and the tech bubble bursting caused the S&P 500 to generate negative returns.

Here's a chart that shows what these losses looked like from 2000 to 2012:

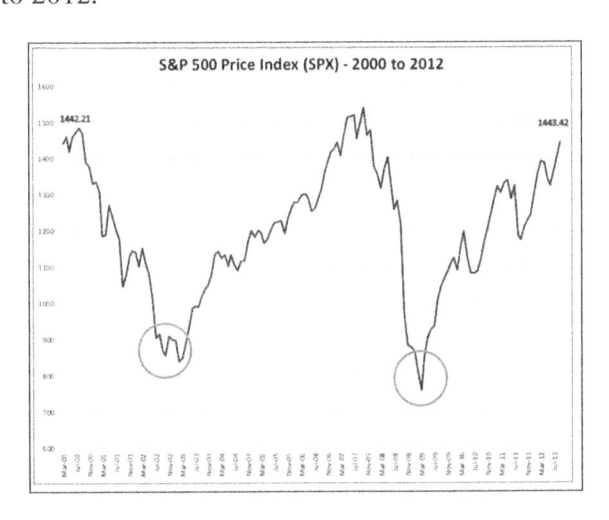

We know people whose retirement plans were destroyed by this downturn. Some canceled plans to retire, while others carefully watched every penny they spent. Others were forced to return to work to make up for the assets the markets had taken from them.

When you are taking withdrawals from your portfolio, the order or the sequence of investment returns can significantly impact your portfolio's overall value.

THE SEQUENCE OF RETURNS MAKES A BIG DIFFERENCE

Here's another way to paint the picture. Let's take two retirees, Mary and Bob, who retire from the same company with the same retirement savings but experience drastically different returns because of the sequence of returns.

Mary and Bob plan to draw 5 percent, or $50,000 annually, from their million-dollar portfolios. They also experience good and bad years, and both achieve the same average annualized rate of return: 4.23 percent.

But look at what a difference timing makes.

In Mary's case, she started retirement during two boom years for the markets. Her portfolio grew 28 percent in year one and 25 percent in year two. Even though the decade ended with two bad years, with losses of 20 percent and 25 percent when that decade was done, she still had $1.1 million for retirement.

Bob experienced the same gains and losses but in a different order. His 20 percent and 25 percent losses happened during his first two years of retirement, wiping out a significant chunk of the savings and leaving him with only $519,758 that he depended on for his future.

And even though he also had two great years of 28 percent and 25 percent growth, these good years came later, after his assets had already been significantly depleted by the bad years. When the ten years was done, he had only half a million dollars to Mary's $1.1 million. In Bob's case, his portfolio could not recover its value, putting him at risk of running out of money much sooner than expected.

This chart shows why the sequence of returns matters. When investors draw money from their portfolios, the order in which they experience gains and losses is often more important than the size of the gains and losses themselves.

	Mary	Annual Return	Bob	Annual Return
Beginning Value	$1,000,000	28%	$1,000,000	-25%
Year 1	$1,230,000	25%	$700,000	-20%
Year 2	$1,487,500	9%	$510,000	12%
Year 3	$1,571,375	14%	$521,200	8%
Year 4	$1,741,368	12%	$512,896	5%
Year 5	$1,900,332	-7%	$488,541	-7%
Year 6	$1,717,308	5%	$404,343	12%
Year 7	$1,753,174	8%	$402,864	14%
Year 8	$1,843,428	12%	$409,265	9%
Year 9	$2,014,639	-20%	$396,099	25%
Year 10	$1,561,711	-25%	$445,124	28%
End Value	**$1,121,283**	**4.23 percent**	**$519,758**	**4.23 percent**

AVOIDING YOUR LOST DECADE

Retirees can't afford to lose a decade of savings growth to large losses. If you were still forty-five or fifty years old with another decade or two to work, save, and rebound, you might be able to recover. But now, when you're sixty-five or older and relying on your retirement to take care of you and fund your dreams, you may no longer have enough time to recover from one bad loss. That's why we want to make sure you're protected from any potential financial cliff.

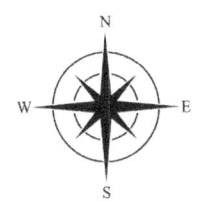

CHAPTER 10

INFLATION HAZARD

A decade ago, some of our clients would grow bored when we warned them about the potential impact of inflation on their retirement portfolios. Back then, inflation rates were relatively low.

But with today's higher inflation rates, we don't encounter much boredom when we discuss this problem now. That's because, in 2024, people experience inflation's impact every time they go to the grocery store or the gas pump.

THE INFLATION CHALLENGE

We tell people to look at inflation as a tax. Uncle Sam doesn't impose it, but as inflation increases, the cost of living also increases, which can eat into your retirement savings and potentially reduce the buying power of your hard-earned money.

Inflation is defined as a measure of the rate at which the general level of prices for goods and services rises and, subsequently, purchasing power falls. To counteract the effects of inflation, it's important to have a retirement plan that takes it seriously, protects you during times of high inflation, and helps your portfolio grow when inflation is low.

VARIED IMPACTS

Inflation can impact your life in retirement, but that impact varies over time, affecting different people in different ways. As you make your way back down the Retirement Mountain, you need to be aware of how vulnerable your personal portfolio is to inflationary pressures.

Historically, inflation rates regularly rise and fall, as we see clearly on the chart below, which provides the last ten years or so worth of data. A quick look at this chart shows that inflation has been relatively stable for a long time, but as we all know, inflation has shot up in recent years.

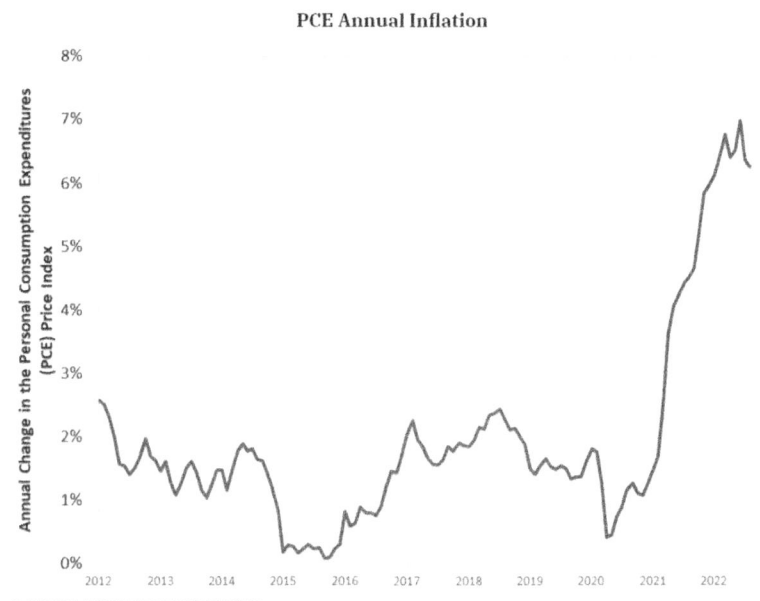

PCE Annual Inflation

■ FEDERAL RESERVE BANK OF ST. LOUIS

SOURCE: Bureau of Economic Analysis.

It's also important to realize that inflation isn't a monolith that impacts everyone similarly. Even though there's a national inflation rate, your experience with inflation will depend on your personal spending and where your dollars go.

As I'm writing this chapter in early 2024, inflation has caused the cost of food and fuel to rise. But the price of used cars and trucks, which skyrocketed in recent years, has settled back down. Likewise, healthcare costs less today than it did six months ago, but it is expected to rise again in the future.

Many of the clients we work with are insulated, at least somewhat, from the impacts of inflation because of their high incomes, high net worth, or reliable pensions. Meanwhile, those retirees with lower and fixed incomes and less savings struggle the most in an inflationary environment.

PART 4

THE DESCENT—
THE SEVEN STEPS DOWN THE RETIREMENT MOUNTAIN

A company that operates hiking and mountain-climbing expeditions warns participants that succeeding in the ascent is just the first half of the climb.

> *"Once you have reached your goal, you need the energy and the ability to walk out after a successful trip."*

The descent can be demanding, but no two mountains have the same gradient or degree of decline. You need to be prepared.

It's the same with your Retirement Mountain.

Retirement is a time of celebration, accomplishment, and relaxation after years of hard work. It is also a time of challenges during the descent phase of your finances—the period we call the distribution phase—when less money is being put into your portfolio, and more money is flowing out.

YOUR RETIREMENT INCOME PLAN

Economic uncertainty and financial stress can diminish the joy of your golden years unless you have a solid retirement income plan. You must navigate the distribution phase of retirement with prudence and foresight as you begin drawing upon your accumulated savings and investments to meet your living expenses.

Retirement income planning can help you do that by focusing on these three challenges you will face on your descent:

1. LONGEVITY

Retirees are living longer than ever thanks to healthcare advances and improved living conditions. That means your distribution phase may last for several decades. This makes it even more important that you and your advisor invest and structure your retirement savings to provide sustainable and reliable income streams that can withstand the test of time.

2. INFLATION AND RISING COSTS

Inflation erodes the purchasing power of money over time. That means you must factor in continually rising living costs. If you don't account for inflation, you could see your retirement years strained by a gradual erosion of your standard of living.

It's not only that gas, groceries, and healthcare cost more. It's that your dollar is worth less across the board. Adequate retirement income planning considers these future expenses and aims to preserve the purchasing power of the income you spent your life generating.

3. MARKET VOLATILITY

Retirees face another risk: market fluctuations. When markets go up and down like a roller coaster, that impacts the value of your investment portfolios.

Worst-case scenario: A significant market downturn early in retirement coupled with withdrawals. This double whammy is a double negative that can severely affect your account balances and future income. (We addressed this risk, called sequence of return risk, in Chapter 9.)

Retirement income planning helps mitigate this risk by diversifying your investments, balancing risk, and ensuring that you enjoy a steady income stream regardless of market conditions.

Prize-winning boxer Mike Tyson said, "Everyone has a plan until they get punched in the mouth."

You can say the same about mountain climbers. Will you be ready when storms or an avalanche hit?

Mountaineers need to plan for bad weather. Retirees need to start with a retirement income plan.

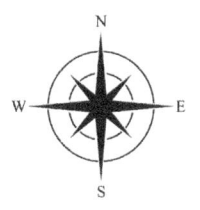

CHAPTER 11

STEP 1—
DEVELOP A RETIREMENT INCOME PLAN AND ROAD MAP

The most significant transition from your working years to your retirement years concerns income. When you are working, you experience a steady inflow of income that covers your expenses and allows you to save for the future. But once you are in retirement, salaries disappear. How will you make up for that missing income?

That's where retirement income planning comes into the equation. It was easy to figure out your income when the payroll checks were regularly flowing in, but it can be much more complicated to figure out what your income will be in retirement when those regular checks cease.

That's why we strongly recommend that people nearing retirement work with an advisor who can help them with their retirement income planning, which is entirely different from standard financial planning. Financial planning focuses on accumulation, while retirement planning focuses on income and distribution.

It takes a different level of experience to help you navigate decades of living during which your primary income stream is shut off.

Your retirement income plan is so important that we view it as a comprehensive, actionable road map that incorporates all your finances into one report. When you build a good plan, you can get an accurate picture of the expected monthly and yearly income you will experience during your retirement years, eliminating guesswork and unnecessary anxiety.

What are your sources of income during retirement? Your retirement income plan will cover them all:

- Social Security

- Pensions

- Annuities

- Brokerage accounts

- 401(k)s and IRAs

- Cash

- Real estate

- Life insurance

- And any additional resources you may have hidden away somewhere

Do you have a written income plan?

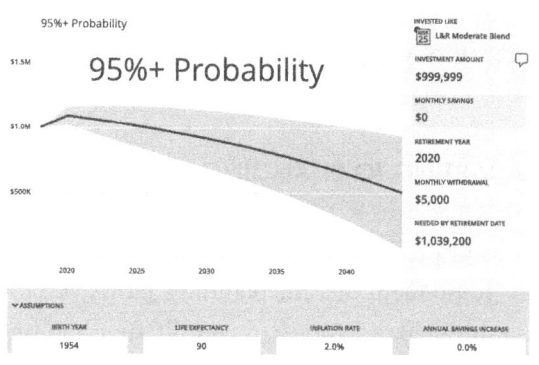

This is a hypothetical example provided for illustrative purposes only; it does not represent a real life scenario and should not be construed as advice designed to meet the particular needs of an individual's situation.

THE FINANCIAL STABILITY THAT BRINGS PEACE OF MIND

Your comprehensive retirement income plan can help you in many ways, but the greatest benefit may be added peace of mind, knowing that you've mapped out a clear strategy for dealing with your expected income, expenses, and financial obligations.

Knowledge is power, and your plan can empower you to make informed decisions, adjust your lifestyle if needed, and avoid unnecessary financial stress from *not* having a plan.

There are three key ways your retirement income plan can help you achieve your goals and enjoy peace of mind.

1. MAXIMIZED RETIREMENT INCOME

Effective retirement income planning aims to maximize the income available during your retirement. By carefully considering all your income sources, you can optimize their cash flow. Your plan will help you figure out the best time to start Social Security and pensions, which accounts to tap first, what percentage to distribute each year from each, annuities and investment portfolios, etc.

This kind of data-driven, strategic approach ensures you get the most out of your hard-earned life savings and investments.

2. ADAPTING TO CHANGING CIRCUMSTANCES

Life is unpredictable. Things can change quickly and unexpectedly. Retirement income planning allows you to adapt to changes with minimal disruption to your lifestyle and financial well-being.

Whether it's unexpected healthcare costs, a new roof, a broken AC unit, family obligations, or economic downturns, a well-structured retirement income plan gives you the flexibility and resilience you will need to navigate challenging times.

3. LEGACY PLANNING AND ESTATE MANAGEMENT

Retirement income planning can cover more than your financial security. Your plan can also provide for legacy planning and estate management. Through proper asset allocation, tax and estate planning strategies, you can pass your wealth to future generations in tax-advantaged ways, support charitable causes, or leave a lasting impact on your loved ones.

ADDING IT ALL UP

When completed, your retirement income plan compiles all this data into one report so you can see your expected monthly and yearly income for the rest of your life in black and white.

Retirement income planning is even more important when

economic clouds have darkened retirement prospects during one of the most daunting times for retirees.

As you made your way up the Retirement Mountain, you passed through numerous bull and bear markets, each impacting your portfolio. Now, as you prepare to return to the base of the mountain, you face stormy weather that's been building for a decade or more.

As we've seen, people are living longer, which means that retirement savings will need to cover more expenses for a longer period of time. Meanwhile, interest rates aren't what they used to be, and markets have been volatile. Through 2022, we had seen over a decade-long bull market in stocks and a surprising thirty-five-year-long bull market in bonds, increasing the risks that millions of Americans could potentially outlive their retirement savings.

Using your retirement income plan as a road map for your journey back down the mountain can help you make necessary adjustments. Many find they need to change their investment approach, taking on less risk to provide greater safety for their existing assets (see Step 4, Chapter 14).

Inflation is another factor you will face on the way down the Retirement Mountain. Recent inflation rates have scared many consumers away from purchases and, over the long term, inflation can negate the growth you experience in your portfolio. A seasoned retirement planner can help you get a handle on how inflation will impact your coming years.

Unfortunately, nearly half of Americans preparing for retirement worry that they won't have enough money to retire. A comprehensive retirement income plan can help them alleviate much of their financial stress.

Carefully following and regularly updating your retirement road map offers added confidence surrounding retirement income. Plus you can have added peace of mind, knowing that a Phase 2 fiduciary retirement planner has mathematically tested your strategy, so your portfolio will last as long as you do.

This way, you can get back to looking forward to your future and all the things you dream of accomplishing in these exciting years, instead of worrying about income, retirement accounts, or changes in the stock market.

CHAPTER 12

STEP 2—
A PLAN FOR SOCIAL SECURITY

You did it for decades: Gave a chunk of each of your paychecks to Uncle Sam for Social Security payroll taxes. A recent estimate said the average American pays $3,045 in payroll taxes yearly. The figure is higher for higher earners.

But did you know that if you make the wrong decision about when to start claiming your Social Security benefits, that decision could cost you hundreds of thousands of dollars in lost benefits during the coming decades?

Retirees must create a plan to maximize Social Security benefits and provide added peace of mind.

There are many factors to consider when deciding the best time to claim Social Security benefits: health, the longevity of family members, current interest rates, and your need for income. Perhaps even more important, how much faith do you have that the system will be around for the rest of your life?

MORE RETIREES ARE LIVING LONGER

America's Social Security Act was passed in 1935, largely as a response to people's widespread losses during the Great Depression.

Government economists set the retirement age at sixty-five, even though Americans' life expectancy at the time was only fifty-eight years. But by 1960, Americans' life expectancy had already soared to almost seventy years. Today, there are nearly forty million retired Americans, many of whom will live into their eighties or nineties.

The first American to receive a Social Security check was Ida May Fuller, a schoolteacher from Vermont. She received her first check in 1937 at the age of sixty-five and received her last check in 1972, the year she died at the age of one hundred.

Her story became a symbol of the positive impact of Social Security on the lives of older Americans, and she made out pretty well overall. The IRS says the taxes she paid into the Social Security program in three years of working totaled only $24.75, while the monthly $22.54 payments she received totaled $22,888.92 at her death. She made out on that deal!

A CHANGING PROGRAM

Social Security was never intended to be a retiree's sole source of retirement income.

The program was only meant to replace 40 percent of working income, but it struggles to cover that much today.

One major change: In the beginning, there were one hundred and sixty workers for every person receiving a check. Today, there are fewer than three workers for every person receiving a check. By 2035, the Social Security Administration will only be able to pay roughly seventy-five cents for every dollar of scheduled benefit. It's unclear if this will eventually reduce benefits by 25 percent.

And what about the so-called Social Security trust fund? It doesn't exist anymore. It has been tapped to pay for other government programs. Currently, Social Security benefits are paid out by current tax revenue, and the agency warns, "We need to resolve these issues soon to make sure Social Security continues to provide a foundation of protection for future generations."

Some have proposed raising the full retirement age to seventy, seventy-two, or even seventy-five to salvage the program. Raising taxes and or ending the cost of living adjustment are also possibilities.

WHEN SHOULD I APPLY FOR SOCIAL SECURITY BENEFITS?

Full Retirement Age (FRA)

- Benefits can start as early as age 62
- Benefits at 62 could mean a benefit reduction of almost 30%
- Maximum benefits are available at age 70
- Benefits roll-up by about 8% per year after full retirement age until 70

Source: https://www.ssa.gov/planners/retire/retirechart.html Accessed: 11.2022

Age To Receive Full Social Security Benefits
(Called "full retirement age" or "normal retirement age.")

Year of birth*	Full Retirement Age
1937 or earlier	65
1938	65 and 2 months
1939	65 and 4 months
1940	65 and 6 months
1941	65 and 8 months
1942	65 and 10 months
1943 - 1954	66
1955	66 and 2 months
1956	66 and 4 months
1957	66 and 6 months
1958	66 and 8 months
1959	66 and 10 months
1960 and later	67

*If you were born on January 1st of any year you should refer to the previous year. (If you were born on the 1st of the month, we figure your benefit (and your full retirement age) as if your birthday was in the previous month.)

YOUR SOCIAL SECURITY STRATEGY: WEIGHING THE PROS AND CONS

Deciding when to start taking Social Security benefits is an important financial decision that can significantly affect your retirement income. Here are three main options people face and the advantages and disadvantages of each.

1. TAKING BENEFITS AT AGE SIXTY-TWO

Pro: You can start receiving benefits when you reach age sixty-two. This option might be suitable if you need the income immediately or have health issues that may reduce your life expectancy.

Con: Taking benefits early will result in a permanent reduction in your monthly benefit amount. If you claim benefits at age sixty-two, your benefit will be reduced by a certain percentage based on your full retirement age (FRA).

2. TAKING BENEFITS AT YOUR FULL RETIREMENT AGE

Your full retirement age is when you become eligible to receive your full Social Security benefit without any reduction. The FRA is typically between ages sixty-six and sixty-seven for most people, depending on the year you were born.

Pro: Waiting until your FRA increases your monthly benefits.

Con: Delaying benefits until your full retirement age means waiting longer to start receiving income. However, waiting until FRA ensures that you receive your full benefit amount.

3. DELAYING BENEFITS UNTIL AGE SEVENTY

Pro: For each year you delay claiming benefits beyond your full retirement age, your benefit increases by a certain percentage, typically about 8% guaranteed and compounded per year. This delayed retirement credit maxes out at age seventy.

Con: Waiting until age seventy means foregoing several years of potential benefit payments. If you have a shorter life expectancy or an urgent need for income, this strategy may not be the best choice.

You and your advisor will want to do the math to find the break-even point in your case. Don't guess or follow the herd. The effort you spend finding a solution that fits your age, health, and life needs will pay off in the long run.

NO ONE-SIZE-FITS-ALL SOLUTION

Everyone's situation is different, but if you are planning on Social Security playing an important role in your retirement years, you could benefit from working with a professional retirement income planner who can help you create a Social Security action plan to determine the best age to start claiming benefits.

Here are some factors to consider as you weigh your options.

Your Financial Needs

Assess your current situation to determine if you can afford to delay Social Security benefits to increase your future payments.

Health and Life Expectancy

Consider your health and family history. Delaying benefits may yield higher lifetime benefits if you expect to live a long, healthy life.

Other Retirement Income

Evaluate other sources of retirement income you may have, such as pensions, 401(k)s, and cash in the bank. This evaluation will help determine if you must rely heavily on Social Security.

Spousal Benefits

If you are married, coordinate with your spouse to optimize both of your Social Security benefits.

Working Status

If you plan to work past your FRA and claim benefits early, be aware that your benefits may be subject to an earnings test limit until you reach your FRA.

WHAT'S BEST FOR YOU?

Our company hosts regular Social Security classes—one client was surprised by what he learned.

"You know, until coming to this class, I always thought taking Social Security at seventy years old is best for everyone, hands down," he said. "Now, after attending your session, I see that there are many other things to consider."

"Exactly," I said. "That's the problem with generic advice. It doesn't fit everyone. Everyone needs to get a customized strategy that will meet their needs."

Monthly Benefit Amounts Differ Based on the Age You Decide to Start Receiving Benefits

This example assumes a benefit of $1,000 at a fulll retirement age of 67

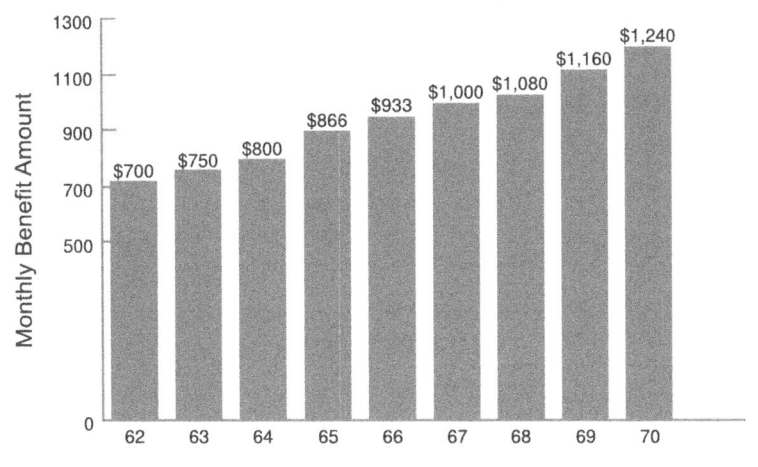

Age You Choose to Start Receiving Benefits	Monthly Benefit Amount
62	$700
63	$750
64	$800
65	$866
66	$933
67	$1,000
68	$1,080
69	$1,160
70	$1,240

BOTTOM LINE

If you take benefits early, you could see a reduction in overall lifetime benefits. But every year you defer taking benefits after full retirement age, your benefit grows by about 8 percent, guaranteed and compounded yearly.

Statistics show that many people claim benefits between the ages of sixty-five and sixty-nine, while only 3 percent of the population waits until seventy. Typically, claiming later makes sense unless you plan to die by age eighty-two. In that case, you would do better by claiming benefits as early as sixty-two.

Many people have paid into Social Security without ever creating an account at www.ssa.gov. Such an account can provide you with a detailed wage history and estimate of available benefits.

We can help you make sense of all this data and make sure you're making the right decisions to maximize your hard-earned Social Security benefits.

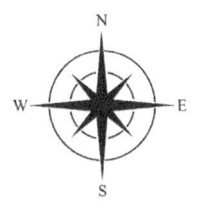

CHAPTER 13

STEP 3—
YOUR WITHDRAWAL AND DISTRIBUTION PLAN

Here's one way to look at your ascent and descent on the Retirement Mountain:

- The ascent is all about accumulation: earning, saving, and investing.

- The descent is all about income: making your accumulated assets work for you for the rest of your life.

Both are important, but have you noticed that most retirement planning advice focuses on the ascent and accumulation? I'm convinced there should be much more focus on the descent side of retirement planning.

You need good advice for both the ascent and the descent, especially if you're just about to retire or have already done so.

Most people we see in our offices don't have an accumulation problem. Mostly, they've done a good job of saving and will have enough to meet their needs, thanks partly to years of great returns.

These people need an income plan: a robust road map that addresses not only income in retirement but also potential threats to that income, including possible future higher taxes, inflation, major market downturns, a healthcare event, and the sequence of returns risk.

BUILDING YOUR RETIREMENT HOUSE

Think of your retirement as a house you will live in for years to come. Building your retirement house is about more than dollars and cents. It's about you, your values, and your convictions.

Building your retirement home requires you to make many complex decisions, and we want our clients to make wise decisions, not foolish ones. This is a subject Jesus addressed when he encouraged people to build their house on the rock, not the sand:

"Everyone who hears these words of mine and puts them into practice is like a wise man who built his house on the rock. The rain came down, the streams rose, and the winds blew and beat against that house, yet it did not fall because it had its foundation on the rock. But everyone who hears these words of mine and does not put them into practice is like a foolish man who built his house on sand. The rain came down, the streams rose, and the winds blew and beat against that house, and it fell with a great crash" (Matthew 7: 24-27).

DETERMINING YOUR INCOME FLOOR

Every house needs a floor and a strong foundation. Your retirement house needs an income floor: a steady source of predictable income that will take care of you when your working paychecks cease and need to be replaced with income from savings.

Your income floor needs to cover all your nondiscretionary expenses—those recurring expenditures to cover the basics of living that you must pay as long as you are alive. Your income floor should be there when you need it, regardless of whether the stock market rises or falls.

Once your income floor is stable, you can focus on walls and a ceiling. This means you have money left over after your basic expenses and can spend some on discretionary purchases you make for fun and pleasure and possibly invest some for more long-term growth.

You need a solid floor to build a stable, long-lasting retirement house. Some of the best floor-building sources are Social Security, pensions, and certain types of annuities. Pre-retirees and retirees should use these sources to create an income floor because they are guaranteed or can be guaranteed for life. (If you don't have a pension, you can use Social Security and annuity income to build the floor.)

Once an income floor is established and nondiscretionary expenses are covered, additional income can come from riskier sources like stocks, bonds, and real estate to cover discretionary expenses.

If your floor is weak, your whole retirement portfolio is shaky. Experience shows that it is very difficult to build this floor during retirement. You need to build it toward the end of the accumulation phase or very early into the distribution phase. But you can continue to work on and adjust the walls and ceiling as you move through your retirement years.

FOUR AIDS FOR THE DESCENT

Descending the Retirement Mountain is all about income: making the assets you accumulated work for you for the rest of your life. Here are four important tools you may find helpful as you live out your retirement years.

1. YOUR WITHDRAWAL STRATEGY

How much can you take out of your retirement portfolio for your life expenses?

Choosing the right withdrawal strategy is crucial to ensure life savings last.

In the 1990s, a popular financial expert introduced the 4 percent rule for systematic withdrawals, dividends from stock portfolios, and annuities. The 4 percent rule is only a general guideline, but it's a good place to start.

Here's the theory. In some years, the markets will do better than 4 percent, and in other years, they won't, but if you never take out more than 4 percent in any given year, you should be OK in the long run.

It is even better to withdraw less than 4 percent annually, cover expenses, and create a surplus unless you don't care about preserving principal and passing money on to loved ones. Most retirees want to preserve principal so that funds are available for healthcare, legacy, unexpected emergencies, etc.

2. YOUR SOCIAL SECURITY STRATEGY

We explored this in Step Two, but it's worth mentioning again. Maximizing Social Security, which means choosing to start benefits at the right time for you, is very important. Making the wrong decision can be costly.

A sixty-five-year-old woman with a monthly benefit of $3,000 will receive well over $1 million in lifetime income if she lives for thirty years. That's a HUGE benefit. You can check it out by running the numbers and figuring out where you will break even.

Consider your current health, family longevity, and other factors when deciding if you need that benefit now or can wait until tomorrow. Make sure you have a professional advisor analyze your particular scenario to see what is best for you.

3. PENSION PLANS

If available to you, this can provide a reliable, guaranteed source of retirement income. However, there are important decisions to be made concerning pension options, lump-sum withdrawals, or annuity payments.

One of our senior retirement planners gave a couple some good news: They had $1.5 million sitting in a pension lump-sum option that they didn't realize they owned. They knew they had "options," but had no idea one option was taking a $1.5M lump sum.

After celebrating this news, they worked together to determine the best decision. They decided to take the lump sum, which made the most sense. Our careful review helped these clients increase their investable assets from $1 million to $2.5 million, which was life-changing. This type of situation, discovering $1.5M, does not happen often; however, this is why it's important to go over all of your options with a Phase 2 fiduciary retirement planner.

4. ANNUITIES

Many people purchase annuities to provide retirement income. Is that a good idea? It depends.

There are good ones and there are bad ones. Some with fees, some without fees. Some are in the market, some are out of the market. Some with the option for guaranteed lifetime income and some that don't have that option.

Work with a fiduciary retirement planner who offers you a variety of options—a toolbox full of items you can evaluate. Sometimes, it takes more than one tool to descend the mountain safely.

You want to build the most appropriate retirement income plan to help you accomplish YOUR objectives, not the advisors'. This is your money, life savings, goals, and dreams. Be aware of the person who wants to sell you something rather than figure out what's best for you.

Annuities are complicated, so I've added a detailed "Annuities 101" sidebar on the next page.

BUILDING A FUTURE THAT'S SOUND

Creating a solid, long-lasting retirement income plan is essential.

Start with a strong floor that supports your retirement income plan, and it will be much easier to build a dependable, predictable and reliable income that will give you added confidence and peace of mind.

ANNUITIES 101: THE FOUR MAIN TYPES

Not all annuities are created equal. Here's a look at the four main varieties.

Immediate Annuities
Industry insiders sometimes call this "your grandparents' annuity" because it was the first kind of annuity product introduced before 401(k)s and IRAs rose to prominence. An employee who worked for a company for some years could earn a pension that would provide regular monthly payments until they passed. Sometimes there was a survivor benefit, sometimes not, but everything ended upon death. But there were no survivor benefits.

One concern: if you put your money into an immediate annuity, it will be locked up forever. You give up all access and control of those dollars forever in exchange for a monthly paycheck.

Over twenty years ago, in my first year in this industry, I was taught that this was "annui-cide." Most people would never want to give up full control of their life savings unless the need for income was extremely high and immediate.

Deferred Fixed
I think of this as a jumbo CD or CD on "steroids." Purchasers get fixed and guaranteed interest for one to five years, typically. Rates currently pay between 4% and 5.5% guaranteed but usually pay between 2% and 3%, which barely keeps up with inflation but is

better than the typical 0% to 2% in the banks. The principal is safe and protected and kept out of the market, so rates are lower. If you have a lot of extra cash in the bank, above and beyond emergency funds, this could be an option to consider, but it may not be the best option for retirement income.

Variable
When critics say something bad about annuities, it's often the variable variety. This product debuted in the 1980s when insurance companies combined insurance with the stock market. Sounds good when markets are up but not when markets are down.

Fees are usually high. Mortality and expense charges, fund costs, bells and whistles added, like guaranteed lifetime income and guaranteed death benefits, can have total annual product costs between 3% and 5%. That's pretty high, but many customers have no clue they're paying that much. Oftentimes these products are sold without the client truly understanding what they've purchased.

Fixed Indexed
Fixed indexed annuities, introduced in 1995, were developed by many of the same companies offering immediate, deferred-fixed, and variables. They were built for people who want the principal protection offered in deferred fixed, but with more upside growth potential, and without the ups and downs of the market and higher fees in variable annuities.

Growth typically comes from "mirroring" a major index without being directly invested in the index. The principal, not growth, is invested in the markets. The positive news is that you can't lose any money when the markets are down. The negative news is you don't have all of the upside either, as in the markets. Nothing that provides all of the upsides with none of the downsides exists.

Fixed-indexed annuities can be great for anyone needing reliable, dependable retirement income. They can also benefit someone looking for a bond alternative in the portfolio that will protect a portion of their life savings and not be subject to the interest rate fluctuations that bonds generate. Still, they provide yields comparable to bonds, usually between 3% to 6%.

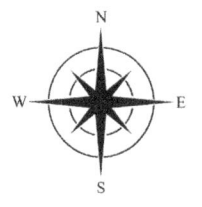

CHAPTER 14

STEP 4—
PROTECT YOUR LIFE SAVINGS

It happens at least once during every mountain climb. You find yourself facing a fork in the path and unsure which one to take.

The same thing happens in retirement, when it becomes increasingly important to keep your portfolio allocated in two different areas:

- Growth opportunities that allow you to increase your portfolio; and

- the income needed to cover your floor of recurring, nondiscretionary expenses.

These two positions shouldn't compete but should complement each other. That's the case whether you opt for the traditional financial planning combination of stocks and bonds, stocks and annuities, or some different combination designed to generate both growth and income.

You want to keep your portfolio growing, particularly during the great years in the market, but with growth comes risk. Anything that can grow by 20 to 30 percent in a good year can lose at least that much in a bad year. Riskier investments let individuals participate in the market's upside potential but offer little to no market downside protection.

Pairing these growth investments with strategies designed to protect funds during market downturns has been championed by Nobel prize-winning economists as a method to create an optimal retirement portfolio.

But as I emphasized above: do not let your accumulation positions compete with your income positions. Keep these two forks in the road separate.

DIFFERENT PURPOSES AND OUTCOMES

Your portfolio should serve your varied needs: growth, income, emergencies, healthcare, and legacy. As you enter retirement, your approach should shift toward income, preservation, and principal protection. Long-term growth is still important, but your emphasis should go from growth to principal protection and preservation.

Retirees who have stopped working and have maxed out their accounts will now fall back on other resources: pensions, Social Security, annuities, rental income, and income generated from investments.

Wise investors will "de-risk" their portfolios by having solutions in place for when the market goes up and when it goes down. After all, such fluctuations happen regularly and are an essential part of a healthy market.

Historically, markets typically go up every three or four years, then correct by contracting. Then they go up again and correct again.

That typical pattern was interrupted by a fourteen-year bull market run from 2008 until the top of 2022. Two unusual factors caused this remarkable run. Interest rates were at rock bottom during these years, we had quantitative easing known as QE, and the government issued more than $7 trillion in stimulus spending during the COVID years. Easy money and historically low interest rates created a scenario where the markets soared, and ushered in the highest inflation in more than forty years.

But don't be caught unaware, as with some people who became overconfident and lost big in the 2008 recession.

An experienced advisor can help ensure your portfolio is truly diversified. Everyone talks about diversification—placing different assets in different types of investments. But confusion remains, some of it caused by advisors who tell clients they are diversified when they're not. Having all of your money in stocks is not the kind of diversification we believe in, although some firms would lead you to believe that it is.

All too often, pre-retirees find out the hard way that most of their money is in one asset class. Diversification isn't simply placing money between large-cap, mid-cap, small-cap, and international stocks. True diversification comes from using multiple asset classes.

THE "RULE OF 100"

Financial folks employ rules of thumb that make it easier to think about diversification. We don't follow these rules to a "t," but they are something to be mindful and aware of, like the 4 percent withdrawal rule. One of these helpful tools is called the "Rule of 100." It's both simple and important.

Here's how it works:

- Start with the number 100. Subtract your current age.

- If you're sixty-five, subtract sixty-five from one hundred.

- Take what's left, in this case 35 percent, and invest that in growth assets while keeping the 65 percent saved for income.

Some retirees may decide they can take on more risk, while others will opt for less. Either way, the "Rule of 100" provides a simple starting point as you seek greater diversification.

We all know that no one should place all their eggs in one basket, but unfortunately, some people have all their eggs in the growth basket without realizing they're doing so.

Pre-retirees take warning: you must regularly review your plan with a fiduciary Phase 2 retirement planner to ensure you are prepared.

In a perfect world, all retirement investments would be protected from major market downturns and principal preserved for the long haul. Everyone would experience steady growth while also distributing income from the investments at the same time.

That's not the world we live in right now. Meanwhile, the world we have is far from perfect. But if you follow proven strategies that incorporate protection of principal while also seeking growth potential, you will fare better than many.

Knowing which fork to take can help you reach your destination healthy and happy.

CHAPTER 15

STEP 5—
BUILD A TAX STRATEGY

One of the biggest myths about retirement is that retirees will be in a lower tax bracket. Some retirees experience higher income—and higher taxes—in retirement than during their working years, thanks to pensions, Social Security, annuity income, rental income, investment income, RMDs, and more.

You have a choice about what you want to do about the retirement tax threat. You can worry about higher taxes tomorrow or create a tax-efficient strategy today.

Who wants to settle for an inferior lifestyle in retirement? Most people work hard toward retirement and don't want to downsize their lives once they get there.

This scenario is typical: When two married people finally retire, they have usually paid off their primary homes. House payments are gone, but so is the mortgage interest deduction. The kids are out of the home, hopefully. No one is working anymore, so there's no more maxing out accounts and contributing to employer-sponsored plans and no more deductions for that.

Many retirees will have less income in retirement, but even they could face similar or higher tax rates than before due to the loss of various deductions.

There are also changes on the horizon. On January 1, 2026, unless something changes between now and then, changes in the tax code will be enacted, with a change in tax brackets and the tax code that may require you to pay more.

For many, taxes will be their biggest retirement expense. This is why you need a tax plan as part of a comprehensive retirement plan that helps you reduce—or at least manage and mitigate—your tax burden as much as possible.

TAXES: HIGHS AND LOWS

Over the last century, Uncle Sam's appetite for taxes has varied. At times during the 1940s and the 1960s, the top tax rate on the highest earners reached an astounding 94 percent, causing some people to ask: what's the incentive for working hard if ninety-four cents of every dollar you earn goes to taxes?

We have it better today, with the highest federal income tax rate being 37 percent. But any tax rate is subject to change.

The good news is that while you can't control what happens to future tax rates or the stock market, you can manage your tax strategy.

Will you pay taxes now? Or later? Or does it make more sense to pursue a combination of both?

OPPORTUNITY KNOCKS

Right now, and through 2025, many federal tax brackets have been reduced, leading to new savings opportunities. Everyone loves a good sale or discount. Thanks to this change, taxes are essentially on sale! Americans have the option to pay federal income taxes at a "discount" on pre-taxed retirement savings plans like 401(k)s, TSPs, SEP IRAs, traditional IRAs, 403(b)s, and 457 plans.

Take a look at the tax chart below. The 15 percent bracket before 2017 is now the 12 percent bracket. The older 25 percent bracket is now 22 percent, and the 28 percent bracket is now 24 percent.

2017	2018 – 2025	2026 - ?
10%	10%	10%
15%	12%	15%
25%	22%	25%
28%	24%	28%
33%	32%	33%
35%	34%	35%
39.6%	37%	39.6%

Most of our clients are in these three brackets, so I will provide an example using these. Suppose you're a married couple earning $200K of taxable income after deductions. You'd be in the bottom of the 24 percent bracket with room to go all the way up to $383,900 without bumping into the 32 percent bracket. In other words, the IRS is telling you that you can make another $183,900 of income and stay in the same 24 percent bracket.

Hello investors! This is a huge opportunity for you to make the most of tax planning, Roth conversions, and the purposeful shifting of assets from pre-taxed accounts into post-taxed accounts can come into the equation.

THE CURRENT FEDERAL TAX CODE

How Important is $1 in Taxes?

- The largest tax bracket jump is from 12% to 22%.
- So, what happens if your income is $22,001 (married, filing jointly) and you move into the next tax bracket by $1?
- The answer is not much. Only the extra $1 into the new tax bracket is taxed at 22%.
- The current tax code will expire in 2026 and revert to 2017 rates, indexed to inflation.

You can also convert these assets into after-tax accounts using permanent life insurance, such as whole life or universal life insurance. If structured properly, these strategies allow you to build up tax-free cash values, access long-term care, and provide tax-free proceeds upon death to your loved ones.

In short, Roth IRAs and permanent life insurance strategies, sometimes known as LIRPs, life insurance retirement plans, are probably the most tax-efficient accounts to pass money on to beneficiaries.

THE MYTH OF LOWER TAXES

Many Americans have most of their retirement nest eggs in pre-taxed accounts, like 401(k)s. After all, they've bought into what we believe is the number-one myth of retirement planning: the myth that when you retire, you'll be in a lower tax bracket because you have less income.

This myth is false for some and harmful to many of our clients and retirees across America. We're telling our clients they may want to take advantage of these temporary savings opportunities. We believe the physical location of your assets is just as important as the asset allocation of your investments.

If all or most of your life savings are in pre-taxed buckets, you could potentially be looking at a ticking tax time bomb if taxes go up in the future, which they more than likely will.

Understandably, Roth conversions are gaining popularity right now. If federal income taxes increase in the future, now may be the best time in recent history to get the most out of pre-taxed dollars before potentially paying higher taxes down the road.

We encourage our clients to run the numbers to evaluate their tax projections. Figure out what your total income is, your total deductions, where you are in the tax bracket, and what your net effective tax rate is. If your total net effective rate for federal and state tax is 20 percent or less, without conversions, you should probably consider conversions, asset shifting, and tax planning.

Some people are even willing to go up to a 25 percent all-in net effective tax rate, including conversions. That means they keep seventy-five cents of each dollar with twenty-five cents to cover taxes. That's fair in our book, but we aim to have twenty cents or less of each dollar going to taxes.

Currently, federal tax rates are historically low, but with over $35 trillion dollars in national debt and climbing, taxes will likely increase. Are you prepared for these changes?

(The growing national debt remains theoretical for many people, but you can make it more concrete by visiting a website that tracks its rise by the second. Visit https://usdebtclock.org/.)

ARE THEY TAXING SEEDS OR THE HARVEST?

One way to understand the impact of taxes on your future retirement is to think about the seed and the harvest.

The Four Tax Buckets

FULLY TAXABLE
- ✓ Pension Income
- ✓ Short-Term Gains
- ✓ Stock Dividends

TAX-DEFERRED
- ✓ Traditional IRA
- ✓ 401(k), 403(b), 457(b)
- ✓ Non-Qualified Annuities
- ✓ Savings Bonds

LONG-TERM CAPITAL GAINS
- ✓ Assets held outside of qualified accounts for more than 12 months

TAX-FREE
- ✓ Roth IRA
- ✓ Municipal Bonds
- ✓ Life Insurance
- ✓ Portion of Social Security Income

Provided for informational purposes only, not intended to provide tax or legal advice or serve as the basis for financial decisions. Your needs, objectives and experience will vary. Consult a qualified tax professional regarding your individual situation.
1 Stock Dividends, may or may not be fully taxable, depending on their character.
2 "Long-Term Capital Gains," it's only capital assets that get capital gains treatment.
3 Roth IRA distributions are only tax-free if the five-year/Age 59 ½ tests are met.
4 Life insurance distributions are only tax-free if its a non-MEC and withdrawals are taken up to basis and loans thereafter AND the contract stays in force until death.

In a Roth IRA, you pay taxes on the seed. Both the seed and it's growth, the harvest, grow 100 percent free of taxation. That's the seed that can bloom and grow into wealth.

But if you have your assets in a standard IRA, the more your assets grow and bloom, the more taxes you will likely pay.

That's why we ask our clients: "Do you prefer to pay taxes on the seed or the harvest?"

If you pay taxes on your seed money before it grows, you can harvest the earnings without any or much tax liability. On the other hand, if you pay no taxes on the seeds and those seeds bloom into a substantial harvest in retirement, you could be looking at serious tax risk and liability if all your eggs are in one tax basket.

Long story short: People pay taxes throughout their lifetimes but never want to pay more tax than necessary. That's even more true during retirement when assets are finite, and the tax man may be cooking up new tax rates to offset the growing national debt and the other fiscal issues the country has.

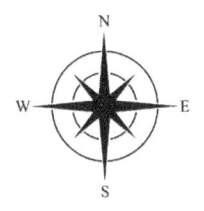

CHAPTER 16

STEP 6—
DON'T FORGET LONG-TERM CARE

Taxes can eat away at your retirement savings bit by bit over the years. However, a long-term medical event during retirement can blow a significant hole in your portfolio.

I've seen this challenge up close. My father's mother lived to nearly ninety-five and needed significant healthcare from age ninety on. During those last four to five years, we could trace her movement:

- From upstairs living to staying downstairs;

- From her own bed to a hospital-style bed;

- From part-time care to full-time care;

- And in and out of hospitals until she eventually passed.

It wasn't easy, and it was expensive. The average cost of a private room in a nursing home today is $8,517 a month. That's over $100,000 a year. How long will your retirement assets last if you need this kind of care?

A COST YOU CAN'T ESCAPE

As of 2022, the average healthcare bill over a lifetime for a married couple in retirement was $315,000. Some assume Medicare and Medicaid will help them, but that's not a sure bet.

There's a common misconception that Medicare covers long-term care. It doesn't.

And to qualify for Medicaid, state-provided healthcare, you must be destitute. Most people need to spend nearly all their assets down to pretty much zero before they can be eligible.

You may convince yourself that you will never need long-term care assistance for in-home care, but statistics don't lie.

We're living longer now; projections tell us that one-third of sixty-five-year-olds living today will live past age ninety. Over the next twenty years, the number of Americans aged sixty-five and older will double to seventy-one million, comprising roughly 20 percent of the U.S. population.

HEALTHCARE

AVERAGE HEALTHCARE BILL FOR A RETIRED COUPLE IN 2022:

$315,000

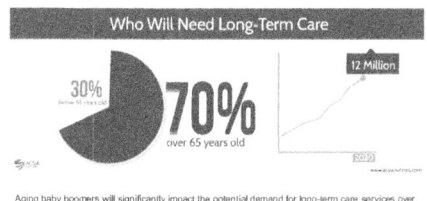

Who Will Need Long-Term Care

30% / 70% over 65 years old

12 Million

Aging baby boomers will significantly impact the potential demand for long-term care services over the next two decades. Over the next 20 years, the number of Americans age 65 and older will more than double to 71 million, comprising roughly 20% of the U.S. population.

Nearly 70 percent of people sixty-five and older will need adult day care or nursing home care. Aging baby boomers will significantly impact the potential demand for long-term care services over the next two decades.

PROTECTING YOURSELF AGAINST A LONG-TERM CARE CRISIS

There are several ways to protect yourself against a long-term care event that can upset your retirement. Here are three common ways to do so.

1. PURCHASE STAND-ALONE LONG-TERM CARE INSURANCE

It is not cheap. Annual premiums average $2,700 a year, but the market is volatile. Many carriers have increased policy premiums by an average of 45 percent, with some rising over 100 percent, leading many retirement advisors to counsel against the purchase of stand-alone long-term care insurance.

Most long-term care providers have dropped out of the market, discontinuing offering the product to new customers and only continuing to provide coverage to existing policyholders.

Most policies have a cost-of-living adjustment because you could potentially pay into a policy for a long time without needing the benefit, only to need it twenty-five years from now when costs are much higher or never needed. Of course, if you need the care, you'll be glad you had a policy, while if you never need the care, you could have paid over $100,000 in premiums over a lifetime that is now down the drain.

A benefit that grows with a cost-of-living increase would be important to ensure your monthly use considers inflation.

While there is a good chance you'll use the policy at some point in your life, there is also a chance you won't. If you don't use it, that money went down the drain all those years you paid premiums.

2. PURCHASE A HYBRID LIFE INSURANCE OR ANNUITY POLICY THAT INCLUDES LONG-TERM CARE BENEFITS

Hybrid policies can be a good alternative or addition to your existing long-term care policy and complement existing long-term care benefits. Most hybrid policies allow a policyholder to use the coverage in several ways, offering more flexibility.

With a hybrid life insurance policy that has an additional rider for long-term care benefits, you can make sure you receive the benefits one way or another: tax-free death benefits to your heirs or in long-term care while you're alive, either in your home, an adult day care facility, or nursing home.

With permanent life insurance designed to last us the rest of our lives, it's guaranteed to pay out one way or the other. If we have a long-term care event and need the funds, we can spend the entire policy down while alive. Usually this is a discounted benefit because money is fronted while alive, but still, you don't have to die to use the policy. And, of course,, the cash value can also be accessed while we're alive.

One type of policy, the living benefit policy, allows you to use monthly benefits for your care. Say you have a policy with a death benefit of $300,000. You can accelerate up to $6,000 of monthly benefit (2 percent of the death benefit monthly) to be used for long-term care or other expenses, as long as you can prove that your conditions keep you from performing the activities essential to daily living. That flexibility is helpful.

These policies usually build cash value that you can withdraw, borrow against, or even use to create a return of premium to get back all the premiums contributed over time in cash value.

Some annuities, usually fixed-indexed annuities, also offer

additional riders for long-term care benefits. They are sometimes called "well-being benefits" or "long-term care doublers." These riders provide one-and-a-half times or even two times the income from the annuity if a healthcare event happens. These leveraged benefits are sometimes offered at no additional cost, but sometimes they may cost an extra 1 percent per year.

3. SELF-INSURING

Retirees who have saved at least $1,000,000 or more may be able to self-insure by setting aside a portion of their nest egg strictly for a potential long-term care event later in life.

This could be part of your bucket approach in retirement:

- A bucket of funds for growth.

- A bucket of funds for income.

- A bucket for emergencies.

- A bucket of funds for healthcare and long-term care.

- And another bucket for legacy if that's important to you.

Whatever you do, make sure you have a plan in place to help insulate you from a future long-term care event. Please don't ignore this or sweep it under the rug, thinking it will never happen to you. Instead, address it head-on and have a plan.

This is one of the biggest risks in retirement, and it can deplete your retirement nest egg quickly.

CHAPTER 17

STEP 7—
PLAN FOR YOUR LEGACY

The previous six steps are important, but don't neglect this last step, which in some ways may be the most important of all: your lasting legacy.

You worked for thirty to fifty years, perhaps. You've lived for seventy, eighty, or ninety years. What will your legacy be? What do you want to continue after you are gone?

Legacy has a lot to do with values, morals, and beliefs about the meaning of life and what you want to leave behind when you go.

What's important to you?

What do you value?

What do you stand for?

What beliefs and values do you want to pass on to the ones you love the most?

We didn't come into this world with anything, and we can't take anything with us when we pass away. As I Timothy 6:7 says,

"For we brought nothing into this world, and it is certain we can carry nothing out."

But even though we brought nothing into this world, we can leave something behind that keeps our values alive and continues our earthly legacy.

Legacy causes us to answer important questions:

Does life have a purpose?

If so, what has been your purpose so far?

Have you fulfilled your purpose?

And what about the future? Do you have a purpose for after you are gone?

DIFFERENT APPROACHES

Life experience shapes people's view of legacy.

In my case, I grew up in a family that had few financial resources. My mom clipped every coupon out of the Sunday paper. My brother and I always had a roof over our heads and always got a new pair of shoes for school, but we had little financial means.

We were raised in a faith-filled Christian home and were shown all the love and support a child could ever want or need to succeed in life. But we grew up with modest means, and I saw the toll that took on our family at times. That's why I want to make sure my family is taken care of financially to the utmost degree when I pass away.

After just six months of working in this business, I made it my mission to help as many people as possible retire with dignity and confidence. Our firm has also taken on that mission: to help people retire with dignity and confidence so they are not in a bad position and need to rely on others for monetary support.

Part of my legacy is to help my family create multigenerational wealth so these monetary and moral values can be passed on to future generations.

You might feel differently. I know many people want to enjoy their hard-earned retirement dollars while still alive. Some even work with an advisor to create a spend-down plan, so when they pass away, their last check bounces!

You may not give a darn about passing money on, and if that's the case, that's OK! It's your money; you've worked for this your entire life, and you should be able to create the plan you want and deserve.

FAITH AND DUTY

I also feel bound by the teachings of my faith, which greatly influences how I see my legacy.

I am grateful that God has blessed me in all areas of my life. I'm married to the world's best wife, and I have the best family, team, and clients. I enjoy the company of many lifelong friends and have a strong support system. And I believe that life is all about giving back. In life, I've seen that the more you give, the more you get back in return, and I want to carry that on even after my life here is done.

I'm determined to build a legacy reflecting my Christian faith and values: Building strong character and standing up for what is right, and working hard. Loyalty. Love of family. Care for people in need. And I'm constantly fine-tuning my plan so it can achieve what I want it to.

WHAT DO YOU WANT YOUR LEGACY TO BE?

There are many ways we help people pursue their legacy goals. Permanent life insurance is one great tool. And estate planning is essential. You can start by setting up a will and trust that directs how your worldly wealth will be distributed. You'll want your assets to be passed on in the most tax-efficient manner possible.

Your plans can ensure that your assets do what you want: Gift your heirs. Fund a grandchild's college education. Pay off a struggling loved one's house. You can be as detailed and specific as you like regarding where your assets go when they pass on, how they pass on, why they pass on a certain way, and how they can be used.

We work hard during our careers to ensure we have enough in retirement. Proper planning allows us to leave beautiful gifts for our families and friends. But with no planning or improper planning, we may leave a nasty legacy of an estate nightmare: court dates, unnecessary attorney fees, family tensions, and time delays.

Please don't do this to your family and loved ones. Take the time to think and plan this out. It's worth it. We've seen what happens when people don't plan, which is not what you want for your family.

Whatever you want your legacy to be, please write it down, work with a professional to put together a plan, and stick with it. Don't neglect to take the valuable time to think through what you would like to happen when you are gone.

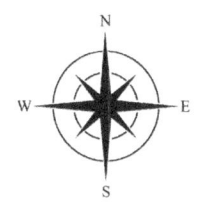

EPILOGUE

EVERYONE HAS AN EVEREST

"Climb Every Mountain," from *The Sound of Music*, is a very inspiring song:

> *Climb every mountain*
> *Ford every stream*
> *Follow every rainbow*
> *'Till you find your dream*

But it would help if you had more than the inspiration to climb a big mountain like Mt. Everest. More than three hundred people have died trying.

Seventy-seven people died in avalanches. You never know what kind of weather will hit you on a mountain.

Seventy-one died in falls, most of those on the descent. "Getting to the top is optional," says famous mountaineer Ed Viesturs, who has summited Everest seven times. "Getting down is mandatory."

Other killers included acute mountain sickness, exhaustion, and exposure. Sometimes, the climb can beat up and wear down even the most experienced climbers.

Perhaps now you can see why my friends and I went "Everesting" together in Utah instead of risking death while spending $50,000 or more each trying to climb the real Everest.

I and a handful of friends had thirty-six hours to climb up and down Snowbasin in Utah until we had gone 29,029 feet, equivalent to the height of Everest.

If we had climbed in Nepal, we would have faced harsh weather conditions. But in Utah, our climbs took place in beautiful weather. It was between sixty and eighty degrees each day.

Even though we had trained for months, "Everesting" was much more difficult than I had imagined. Afterward, I was fatigued but elated. I was in a ton of pain and very sore, but I was super proud of myself for doing what I did.

I learned a ton. I challenged myself, raised the bar, and reached my goal.

HOW'S YOUR CLIMB?

My experience in Utah is similar to what most people experience daily. Instead of making a straight beeline up the mountain of life, most of us climb in stages, experiencing small victories and occasional defeats along the way as we confront each new challenge we face.

Unless you are a RINO (Retired In Name Only), your retirement years won't subject you to the challenges you faced in your career. But your retirement years will bring plenty of other challenges. I want you to be ready to meet those challenges and enjoy all the wonderful things in store.

Climbing on life's mountain is arduous. Reaching the peak is difficult, and the descent back down is potentially even more dangerous.

But once we get out of the dangerous heights and down into the foothills again, the terrain changes, and life appears abundantly. Plants and trees, birds and bees, and perhaps a babbling brook.

WHEN YOU NEED A "RETIREMENT SHERPA"

I've experienced the joy and thrill of reaching difficult goals. Now, I want to spend my life helping you and others do the same. Think of me as a retirement sherpa who can help you tackle your mountain.

Now that you've made the climb up and survived the ascent back down your own mountains in life, a trained retirement sherpa can help you experience the satisfaction and contentment in enjoying the rest of life at a slower, less arduous pace while knowing that you have what it takes to make your retirement years truly golden.

Countless mountaineers inspired me. And a handful of mentors and coaches got me into shape to reach new heights.

Now, I want to come alongside you—wherever you are in your climb right now—and help you take the next step and the step after that until we can celebrate and toast your success.

ARE YOU READY?

Are you prepared to make your way down the Retirement Mountain?

Your experienced financial sherpa can help you safely navigate the terrain and conditions while keeping your personal goals in mind.

Your sherpa can help you make the best decisions in all of the following areas listed on the worksheet on the next page:

APPENDIX

WORKSHEET

INCOME

Five years from today, how do you expect your household annual income to change?

- ☐ To grow substantially
- ☐ To grow moderately
- ☐ To stay about the same
- ☐ To decrease moderately
- ☐ To decrease substantially

TIME

What is your financial time horizon for retiring?

- ☐ Short (less than three years)
- ☐ Medium (three to ten years)
- ☐ Long (longer than ten years)

GOALS

What are your goals within your portfolio?

- ☐ My portfolio is not my primary concern. I'm more concerned with current income.
- ☐ Stay the same or slightly increase

☐ Greater than today
☐ Substantially greater than today

NEEDS

Which of the following challenges do you need help achieving? (Check all that apply.)

☐ Increase my standard of living
☐ Financial security at retirement
☐ Increase my net worth by a certain percentage
☐ Reduce my tax burden
☐ Simplify my tax burden
☐ Pay for college education for children
☐ Provide for my family in the event of my death
☐ Minimize the cost of probate and estate taxes
☐ Control the distribution of my assets to my heirs
☐ Plan for home healthcare/nursing home care

OBJECTIVES

What are your specific financial objectives?

☐ Income now
☐ Guaranteed interest rate
☐ Probate avoidance
☐ Growth (long-term)
☐ Pass assets to beneficiaries at death
☐ Future income
☐ Potential interest based on market
☐ Tax-deferral

☐ Lifetime income
☐ Other

INCOME GOALS

How much income do you want from your portfolio during your retirement years ($/year)?

OTHER GOALS

Are there goals you want to make sure you plan for?

OTHER CONCERNS

If you could change two things about your current financial situation, what would you change?

You have many options before you, which means you have many choices to make.

Knowing your goals and expectations will make your journey down your Retirement Mountain as rewarding as your climb up.

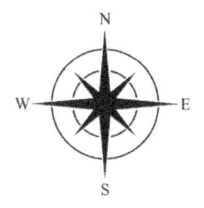

ABOUT THE AUTHOR

Abe founded Abich Financial Services (AFS) in 2008 and has over twenty years of experience in financial services. He is a seasoned retirement income planning professional and a Certified Financial Fiduciary®.

Abe hosts the D.C. metro area radio show, "The Retirement Key," on 105.9 WMAL and the television show, "The Retirement Key," on NBC4, ABC7 WJLA, and WUSA 9.

Abe and the team have helped over a thousand individuals and families prepare for their financial futures and retire with dignity and confidence. His authored articles can be seen in *Forbes*, *Fortune*, Yahoo! Finance, CNN Money, and more. Abe has also served as a member of the *Forbes* Financial Council. He earned his B.S. from Liberty University, where he lived out his dream to pitch for their Division I baseball team.

In August 2015, Abe married his wife, Shelly, and they became proud Leesburg residents and teamed up to run AFS as a family firm. With a determination to always give back to the local community, he joined his wife in starting a senior nonprofit, the Love of Gray. Abe has served on the board for Loudoun Habitat for Humanity, and is a member of the Loudoun County Chamber of Commerce and regularly attends Cornerstone Chapel in Leesburg. He is a die-hard Washington Commanders fan and, on weekends, enjoys being a local foodie, running and hiking the trails, boating on the Potomac and participating in endurance events like 29029 Everesting and ultra marathons.

Take Your First Step Down Your Retirement Mountain

Schedule a complimentary appointment with us:

Abich Financial Services
20135 Lakeview Center Plaza Suite 110
Ashburn, VA 20147

www.abichfinancial.com/book

Call us at: (571) 577-9968

Made in the USA
Middletown, DE
04 September 2025